Missions Moments 2

52 Easy-to-Use Missional Messages and Activities for Today's Family

Mitzi Eaker

Birmingham, Alabama

New Hope® Publishers
P. O. Box 12065
Birmingham, AL 35202-2065
www.newhopepublishers.com

New Hope Publishers is a division of WMU®.

© 2008 by Mitzi Eaker.
All rights reserved. First printing 2008.
Printed in the United States of America.

No part of this publication may be reproduced, stored in a retrieval system, or transmitted in any form or by any means—electronic, mechanical, photocopying, recording, or otherwise—without the prior written permission of the publisher.

Library of Congress Cataloging-in-Publication Data

Library of Congress Cataloging-in-Publication Data

Eaker, Mitzi, 1972-
　Missions moments 2 : 52 easy-to-use missional messages and activities for today's family / Mitzi Eaker.
　　p. cm.
　Includes bibliographical references (p.171-172).
　ISBN 978-1-59669-210-7 (sc)
　1. Family--Prayers and devotions. 2. Family--Religious life. I. Title.
BV255.E25 2008
249--dc22
　　　　　　　　　　　　　　2008010537

All Scripture quotations, unless otherwise indicated, are taken from the HOLY BIBLE, NEW INTERNATIONAL VERSION®. NIV®. Copyright © 1973, 1978, 1984 by International Bible Society. Used by permission of Zondervan. All rights reserved.

ISBN-10: 1-59669-210-3
ISBN-13: 978-1-59669-210-7

N087101 • 0808 • 3M1

Praise for Missions Moments 2

"*Missions Moments 2* is another great tool to help churches impact the next generation with God's heart for the world! It's so user friendly for the pastor doing a children's sermon, the teacher presenting a brief missions message, or the parent leading a family devotion time. *Missions Moments 2* covers another wide range of missions topics in bite-size pieces so children can easily understand God's heart for the nations. These 52 easy-to-use presentations will get kids excited about their world and how God wants to use them."

—**Jill Harris**, Kidzana Ministries

"Incredible material! As I was reading through these lessons, I was thinking, *Wow! God can use children to share the love of Christ too!* Mitzi has done an excellent job of incorporating biblical learning, prayer, evangelism, and missions into 52 age-appropriate drop-in lessons for the purpose of instilling within children a missional lifestyle. And that's not all. One of the greatest benefits to this book is that it encourages family participation. What better place to develop a missional lifestyle than in the home! If you are involved in the spiritual development of children, whether in the church, school, or home, then I highly recommend this book. These lessons are easily adaptable for any setting and would be a great asset to your ministry to children."

—**Skip Arnhart**, North American Mission Board

"Families today are looking for tools that help bring them together with purpose. *Missions Moments 2* provides opportunities to encourage and develop missional thinking and response. Mitzi Eaker again has done an excellent job of gathering 52 Bible stories and appropriately tying them together with fun, interactive learning opportunities."

—**Bill Emeott**, lead childhood ministry specialist, LifeWay Christian Resources

"Never has fostering both family commitments and a call to missions been more needed. Mitzi Eaker's *Missions Moments 2* does both at

once. Winsome, clear, passionate…this book will shape the hearts of daughters and sons for God's world and all peoples—beginning at home and church."
—**Carey C. Newman**, PhD, director, Baylor University Press

"In *Missions Moments 2*, Mitzi Eaker has provided ideas that are very easy to implement. All of the ideas are biblically based and materials needed are easy to secure. An extra bonus is Bible memorization. They can certainly be used in church but are also excellent for parents teaching their children about missions."
—**Lezlie Armour**, children's minister, Champion Forest Baptist Church, Houston, Texas

Table of Contents

Acknowledgments. 10
How to Use This Book 11

I   Foundations of Faith. 13
    1   Family 15
    2   Community 18
    3   Creation 21
    4   Abraham. 24
    5   Babel 27
    6   Moses—Depending on God. 29
    7   Moses—Following God's Plan 32
    8   David 35
    9   Esther. 38
    10 Isaiah 41
    11 Jesus—Christmas. 43
    12 Disciples. 46
    13 Jesus—Easter. 48
    14 Paul 50
    15 Antioch. 52
    16 Holy Spirit 55
    17 Heaven 58

II   Foundations of Missional Living 61
    18 Active Compassion 63
    19 Mission Action. 66
    20 Following Jesus 69
    21 Knowing God. 72
    22 Loving God 75
    23 Loving Others 78
    24 My Purpose 81
    25 My Part. 83
    26 My Time. 86
    27 My Talents 89

- 28 My Money ... 92
- 29 My Tithe. ... 95
- 30 My Speech ... 97
- 31 My Testimony ... 100
- 32 My Friends. ... 103
- 33 Go to People. ... 106
- 34 Go to the World ... 109

III Missions ... 113
- 35 Missions Education ... 115
- 36 Missiology ... 118
- 37 Missionaries. ... 121
- 38 Church Planting ... 124
- 39 Evangelism. ... 127
- 40 Partnership Missions ... 130
- 41 Technology. ... 133
- 42 Children ... 136
- 43 Animals ... 139
- 44 THUMB. ... 142
- 45 THUMB: **T**ribal Peoples ... 146
- 46 THUMB: **H**indu Beliefs ... 149
- 47 THUMB: **U**nreligious People ... 152
- 48 THUMB: **M**uslim Beliefs ... 155
- 49 THUMB: **B**uddhist Beliefs ... 159
- 50 Moldova. ... 162
- 51 Indonesia ... 165
- 52 South Africa. ... 168

Resources ... 171
Topical Index. ... 173

Dedication

This book is dedicated to my precious son,
Evan, to baby Eaker, who is due
at the release of this book,
and to my amazing husband, Shane.

Acknowledgements

I would like to thank my family—Shane and Evan Eaker; Larry and Martha Gibbs; Granny Gibbs; Shawn, Amy, Micah, and Lydia Gibbs; Gayle and Gary Eaker; Rob, Katie, Joshua, and Andrew—and friends Kristi Griem, Denise Roebuck, and Tina Atchenson for their support through the process of writing *Missions Moments 2*. I'm grateful for the prayers and support from our Sunday School class and Girls in Action® leaders at Dawson. I'm overwhelmed by my church families at Slackland, Southside, and Dawson who have supported my ministry through various stages of life. I'm indebted to the Children's Resource Team at national Woman's Missionary Union (WMU) for your encouragement and sharpening over the years. I love WMU! Thank you to the staff at New Hope Publishers and to Andrea Mullins who saw the potential in me for a ministry consultant and writer before I could believe it myself.

This book would not have been possible without the support and understanding of my husband, Shane. I love you, Shane! And of course, thank You, God, for working through me despite my own inabilities and shortcomings. Thank You, Jesus, for Your love and grace!

My hopes for *Missions Moments 2* are threefold:

- That parents will use the book as a tool to draw their families closer to God as they talk to their children about faith and missions.
- That churches will use the book to introduce children to the biblical basis of missions and missional living.
- That teachers will use the book for ideas on making the concept of missions real to the children.

How to Use This Book

Missions. What comes to mind when you think of the word? And what does it mean to "do missions"? We use these words often, but do we know what they mean?

One of our greatest challenges and charges is to make missions not just a lofty concept or something other people do, but a reason to pray and act to promote God's kingdom. This book's chapters will supply you with both biblical background and practical suggestions to inspire and energize children and their families in carrying out Jesus's charge to spread the gospel into all the world. You'll find you can use the information in this book in these ways and others:

Use for Children's Sermons
Share Making It Real. Make copies of Making It Personal and Making It Home to give to the children or print in the church bulletin for the child and family to do at home.

Use for Family Devotionals
Create a year-long family missions emphasis. Give the book to each family to use for their weekly devotionals. Plan monthly or quarterly family events, including ministry projects, to motivate families to use the book throughout the year.
Share Making It Real. Lead the children through Making It Stick. Debrief with Making It Home. Give the children the Making It Personal challenge to do throughout the week.

Use for Missions Drop-In
Share Making It Real. Lead the children through Making It Stick. Teachers can make copies of Making It Personal and Making It Home for the child and family to do at home.

Additional Uses
- Add music and hands-on activities for children's worship.
- Provide as a missions learning supplement in children's curriculums.

- Drop-in missions learning experiences.
- Use in Christian school and homeschool settings to teach the biblical basis of missions.
- Use selective messages for missions projects preparation for families, children, and preteens.

Message to Parents

God has given you a unique and awesome opportunity to raise children to have a relationship with God and a life dedicated to serving Him. You are journeying and learning as a family about God grace, love, and faithfulness through God's Word, and how to respond to life experiences. *Missions Moments 2* is designed to provide a series of messages and learning reinforcement activities for families to use on their journey. It allows you to talk about biblical messages of Christian living, serving God, and ministering to others.

The "Taking It Home" segments in each chapter ask probing and challenging questions to encourage family members to share biblical beliefs and personal faith experiences. Each chapter also calls the family to personal or social action through a suggested witnessing or mission action idea. This helps reinforce a biblical worldview in the hearts and minds of your children as they apply the Bible to their lives and put their faith into action.

Make *Missions Moments 2* work for your family's schedule; it contains 52 weeks of devotionals—one for each week of the year. You can set aside a night once a week following dinner to have family time. However, your family may decide to do the devotional more or less often. Consider journeying through *Missions Moments 2* with other families in your church. This can be done by starting the book at the same time and meeting with other families once a month or quarter to do a ministry project together and discuss what your have learned through the book's messages.

For resources on guiding your children spiritually and to share how your family is using *Missions Moments 2* and doing missions, see the Resources section at the end of this book and visit www.MitziEaker.com.

1
Foundations of Faith

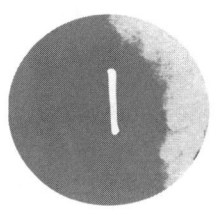

Family

Missional Message: God wants families to serve Him.

Missional Challenge:
"Only be careful, and watch yourselves closely so that you do not forget the things your eyes have seen or let them slip from your heart as long as you live. Teach them to your children and to their children after them."
—Deuteronomy 4:9

"I have been reminded of your sincere faith, which first lived in your grandmother Lois and in your mother Eunice and, I am persuaded, now lives in you also."
—2 Timothy 1:5

What Is Needed: Bible, pictures of families from around the world, copies of letter addressed to parents for the children to take home with them

Making It Real

(*Show pictures of families from around the world—magazines, photo essay books, and children's textbooks are good sources.*)

Do you know that families have a very important place in the Bible? Stories about families are found in the very first book of the Bible, called Genesis. That's where we read about Adam, Eve, and their two sons Cain and Abel. Children often learn about God in their families.

There are many other places in the Bible that talk about grandparents, parents, and children. Deuteronomy 4:9; 2 Timothy 1:5; and Ephesians 6:4 show how the parents and even grandparents have an important role in teaching their children and grandchildren about God.

In the New Testament, Paul tells of how Timothy was influenced by the faith of his mother and grandmother. (*Read 2 Timothy 1:5.*) Paul was saying that Timothy's grandmother and mother did an excellent job teaching Timothy.

Think about it. You know your family better than you know anyone else. Your family influences who you are. For example, in the mornings when the family is getting ready for church, if someone wakes up grouchy, the sour mood can spread to the whole family. However, if family members get up excited about worshipping God and their morning is filled with anticipation about going to church, then the family will have a better day.

What if, every day, families woke ready to serve Jesus? I think we could change our communities if families began their days with Jesus.

In fact, families could change the world! What if every family not only woke up every morning filled with joy at following Jesus, but then went into the community and ministered to others? If every Christian family began working together to make a difference for Jesus—first, in their family, second, in their community, and third, in the world—we would change the world.

Children, take time this day to discuss with your family how you can start the day with Jesus. And begin doing so.

Prayer

God, thank You for my family. Guide our family and the other families in our church to learn more about You and to share what they learn with others.

Making It Stick

Have children brainstorm possible family ministry projects. Examples might be making cards for soldiers stationed overseas, participating in a cleanup day at your neighborhood park, or leading a short worship service at a nearby retirement home, but there are many other possibilities. Help make the project realistic. Send a pre-written letter home with the children to encourage their families to implement a project.

Making It Personal

Memorize Deuteronomy 4:9.

Make time for your parents or grandparents to teach you about the Bible. This week study the Bible with your parents or grandparents. Ask them to share with you how God has worked in their lives.

Making It Home

Choose a Scripture verse as your family's motto and post it where everyone can see it often. Set aside family time every morning this week to start the day with Jesus. Implement the family ministry project that your child has created.

Community

Missional Message: God's church has a divine purpose.

Missional Challenge:
"Now you are the body of Christ, and each one of you is a part of it."
—1 Corinthians 12:27

What Is needed: Bible, blackboard or dry erase wipe board, poster board, and markers

Making It Real

In the beginning, God created man. He said it is not good for man to be alone, so He created woman. God was very pleased with His creation (Genesis 1:27–31; 2:18).

Since the beginning of time, God has created billions of people! Today there are more than 6 billion people alive. *(Write "6,000,000,000" on a blackboard or dry wipe board. If you have access to a computer, you can look up the exact figure at:*

http://www.census.gov/ipc/www/popclockworld.html.) God's purpose has not changed. God's purpose is fellowship with His creation and for people to bring honor to Him through their lives. To fulfill God's purpose, He has called us to be His people. He wants us to live in community with Him and other believers who follow Him so that we can help bring others to God (Matthew 5:14–16; 28:18–20).

God first chose a people from a part of the world that we now call "The Middle East" to be His community. He gave those people, who came to be known as "the Israelites," laws to live by. They were a community that believed in God. They followed the Word of God together and taught the Bible to their children and their children's children (Deuteronomy 5:1–21; 7:6; 11:18–21).

Today, God's community extends beyond the Israelites to us (Acts 10:44–45). God's community includes those who follow Christ, sometimes called "Christ followers" or "Christians" or "the church." In Acts 1:8, before Jesus went to heaven, He gave instructions to His followers to be His witnesses to the entire world. The followers of Christ, the church, are to be God's representatives of Jesus to the world.

First Corinthians 12:27 says that we are the body of Christ, the church, and each one of us has a part. God has given each of us a special role and a responsibility.

Think about all the people you know that are followers of Jesus. Look around at the people in your church. The believers in your church are just a small part of the whole, the countless other believers in the world who make up God's people, the church.

God wants all of His people to work together as a community to follow God's teachings found in the Bible; this includes behaving like Jesus to all peoples of the world.

Prayer

God, thank You for our church. Help it to work together and live in a way that all people will come to know Jesus. Help me to fulfill my role in spreading the good news to people who have not yet heard it.

Making It Stick
Read or reread Acts 1:8; 1 Corinthians 12:27; Acts 2:42–47; and Ephesians 1:22.

What does the Bible say about following Jesus and about the church community?

Prior to the lesson, ask a pastor at your church to drop in on the class for five minutes at the end of the lesson time. Before that, have the children write their responses to this question on a piece of poster board. When the pastor comes in, let the children share their ideas and suggestions.

Making It Personal
Memorize 1 Corinthians 12:27.

What does being a part of the church mean to you? Think of several ways that you can be part of the work of the church. Give your time this week to do some of these activities.

Making It Home
As a family, discuss how your family is part of the church. Brainstorm ways to daily apply 1 Corinthians 12:12–27 to your family's role in the body of Christ.

Creation

Missional Message: God instructs us to care for the earth.

Missional Challenge:
"Then God said, 'Let us make man in our image, in our likeness, and let them rule over the fish of the sea and the birds of the air, over the livestock, over all the earth, and over all the creatures that move along the ground.'"
—Genesis 1:26

What Is Needed: Bible, flowering plant for illustration, water, glass, seeds or flowering plants for each child, potting soil, and pots

Making It Real
(*Show children a flowering plant in a glass of water without soil, so that children can see the root system.*)

God created this plant. He created roots to help it grow. God created plants like this one to provide oxygen. Oxygen helps us to breathe. God created the earth with the resources that humans need to live.

Do you think God cares about how we treat the earth?

In the beginning, God took great care in how He created heaven and earth. And He was very proud of His creation. God also created humans and gave them rule over the earth. This means that God gave each of us the responsibility to care for the earth (Genesis 1).

God created earth in such a way that it has everything needed to keep humans, animals, and plants alive. We eat the food that the earth provides. We breathe in the oxygen that the earth provides. We live with the water the earth provides. We consume the natural resources of the earth.

God cares how we treat the earth. That is one of the responsibilities that He has given to us. When we do not take care of the earth, we are neglecting our responsibility to God. We honor God when we care for all that He has given to us, including the earth.

Prayer
God, thank You for giving us a wonderful place to live. Please help us to care for the earth You created.

Making It Stick
Discuss with the children why God wants us to take care of the earth. Have each child list ideas of how he or she can take care of the earth and and how they can encourage others to do the same. Let children plant the seeds or flowers in the pots and soil you have provided. Tell the children how to care for the plants. Encourage children to take their plants home and to take care of them.

Making It Personal
Memorize Genesis 1:26.

Look around your home and community and discover ways that you can take care of the earth where you live. Commit to do at least one thing to care for the earth.

Making It Home

What is your family doing to care for the earth? Discuss ways that your family can take care of the world God gave us to live in. Consider ways that you can conserve energy, recycle resources, and reduce waste. Plant a tree to signify your family's commitment to caring for the earth.

Abraham

Missional Message: We must be obedient to God's leading.

Missional Challenge:
"By faith Abraham, when called to go to a place he would later receive as his inheritance, obeyed and went, even though he did not know where he was going."
—Hebrews 11:8

What Is Needed: Bible, child or adult volunteer, construction paper for cards, and markers

Making It Real
(Before the lesson ask a child or church staff member to help you.)
Hello, boys and girls. I have asked _____ to help me today. *(Ask the volunteer to stand up and close his eyes.)* Now I am going to lead you, _____, with my voice. *(Use voice directions to lead the volunteer around a few safe obstacles for about one minute, guiding the volunteer for additional safety as needed.)*

(*Ask the volunteer how it felt to be led around without knowing where he or she was going.*) It can be pretty exciting and scary to follow in this way. How many of you would have wanted to peek, to see where you were going?

The Bible tells us in Hebrews 11:8 that Abraham was obedient to God and followed God even though he did not know where he was going. The story of God's first instructions to Abraham is told in Genesis 12. God came to Abraham and told him to leave his country, his people, and his father's household and to go to the land to which God would lead him.

Abraham followed God. Abraham could have said, "Thanks, but no thanks. I am happy just where I am." Instead, Abraham followed God and obeyed what God told him. God promised to bless Abraham. We learn that Abraham was obedient to follow God, and God kept His promise to Abraham.

Prayer
God, help us to obey You and follow where you lead us, like Abraham.

Making It Stick
Read Genesis 12:1–5. Sometimes God asks us to give up things to follow Him. Lead children to discuss how hard it would be to leave where they live and go into a foreign country. Describe how missionaries leave their homes to follow God. Pray for missionaries as they follow God to go to different places around the world to tell others about God. Create and send encouragement cards to missionaries whom your church supports.

Making It Personal
Memorize Hebrews 11:8.

Make a list of the items you have or activities you participate in that would be hard to do without, such as TV, video game, computer, and cell phone. Give up one or more of the items on your list this week. Take the time that you would have spent on these other activities to pray, asking for God to guide you in where He wants you to go and how He wants you to spend your time.

Making It Home

Have family members jointly compose a list of the top ten items around the house they consider to be most important. Discuss how hard it would be to give up those items. As a family, agree to give up a certain number of the items on your list for one week. At the end of the week, talk about what you have learned. Also, discuss the fact that many families in the world do not even have access to most of these items and would think of them as luxuries, not necessities.

Babel

Missional Message: God wants us to trust Him.

Missional Challenge:
"Trust in the LORD with all your heart and lean not on your own understanding."
—Proverbs 3:5

What Is Needed: Brick, construction paper, and markers

Making It Real
Today I brought something to show you. It is a brick. What do we do with bricks? Build walls, build buildings, and such. There are many stories in the Bible about using bricks to build. The first story of using bricks is found in Genesis chapter 11. (*Read Genesis 11:1–9.*)

You see, the people had this idea to use bricks to build a city for themselves and a tower to reach to heaven. The people wanted to bring attention and glory to themselves. They wanted to do things their own way without God. However, God stopped their plan by making everyone speak different languages. They were not able to understand each other and so they so they were unable to work with one another. After this, the people scattered throughout the earth. God knew that no matter how high they built the tower, they would not be able to get to Him or heaven. He wanted the people to learn that they could not trust their own knowledge and strength, but to learn they had to trust Him.

We learn from this story that God wants us to trust Him and not to do things our own way. God's Word says in Proverbs 3:5, *"Trust in the LORD with all your heart and lean not on your own understanding."* God's plan is for us to trust Him.

Prayer
God, thank You for being with us always. Help us to trust You and Your ways each day of our lives.

Making It Stick
Have each child draw a brick or two on construction paper—red, gray, or brown are good choices—or have pre-drawn brick patterns ready. Have them cut out their bricks and write on them a thing they do that shows they trust in God rather than relying on their own understanding and strength. If you have more time, discuss how the wide variety of languages in the world make it essential for missionaries to trust God, rather than their own knowledge, to communicate for them.

Making It Personal
Memorize Proverbs 3:5.

Take some of the bricks that represent how you need to trust God. Hang them in a place that you see daily. Review them every morning, so you will remember throughout each day to trust God.

Making It Home
Discuss ways in which Proverbs 3:5 relates to your family trusting God. Hold one another accountable this week to seek God for understanding and strength.

Moses— Depending on God

Missional Message: God wants us to depend on Him.

Missional Challenge:
"You shall speak to him and put words in his mouth; I will help both of you speak and will teach you what to do."
—Exodus 4:15

What Is Needed: Poster with a front side heading saying "God's Words" and back side saying "Moses's Question," additional poster board, or a dry wipe board, markers

Making It Real

How many of you have seen a movie or read a story about Moses? Raise your hand if you think Moses was a great man. Let me tell you a story about when Moses first met God, as found in the Bible in Genesis 3. God came to Moses in the form of a voice and a burning bush one day when Moses was out in the field tending the sheep. (*After each of God's statements, hold up the sign to show* "God's

Words." *After each of Moses's questions, turn the sign to show the big* Q *and* "Moses's Questions.")

God	God spoke to Moses saying, "Moses go to Pharaoh, the King of Egypt, and request that he free the Israelites from slavery." (Display "God's Words.")
Moses	(*Display Moses's Questions.*) Moses questioned saying, "Who am I to go and do this?"
God	God replied, "I will be with you." (Display "God's Words.")
Moses	(*Display Moses's Questions.*) Moses questioned, "Who do I tell them You are?"
God	God said, "Tell them I am the God of your fathers.
Moses	(*Display Moses's Questions.*) Moses questioned, "What if they do not believe me?"
God	God then showed him miracles that he could use to prove that he was sent by God. (Display "God's Words.")
Moses	(*Display Moses's Questions.*) Yet Moses stated: "But, God, I am not a good speaker."
God	God told him, "I will speak through you." (Display "God's Words.")
Moses	(*Display Moses's Questions.*) Moses asked last, "Can You please just send someone else?"
God	God said, "I will speak to you, and Aaron can speak for you to Pharaoh." (Display "God's Words.")

After five times questioning God, Moses finally left to do what God instructed him to do.

After hearing this story, raise your hand if you think Moses was a great man. The truth is that God worked through Moses to make him great. In Exodus 4:15, God says, *"I will help both of you speak and will teach you what to do."*

The rest of Moses's life, he tried hard to follow God's leadership. Sometimes Moses struggled to follow God, but God always helped him when it was hard. Moses depended on God to lead him.

Prayer
God, thank You for always being there to show us what we need to say and do.

Making It Stick
Write these phrases on a poster board or dry wipe board. (You can have them ready prior to class, if desired.)
- Why me?
- Who are You?
- Why will they believe me?
- But, I cannot speak.
- Can You send someone else?

Lead children to state why Moses would have used these phrases. Also, list additional phrases that children use when they believe they cannot do something. Explain how God wants us to depend on Him. Use the list to close in prayer asking for guidance from God in each situation.

Making It Personal
Memorize Exodus 4:15.

Make a list of the excuses you use not to follow what God says in the Bible. Pray that God will show you how to depend on Him to do what He is leading you to do.

Making It Home
Share with your children an instance when you felt God leading you to do something but you had to depend on Him for guidance and maybe even for words. Teach your children Philippians 4:13.

Moses— Following God's Plan

7

Missional Message: God gives us plans and instructions.

Missional Challenge:
"Let love and faithfulness never leave you; bind them around your neck, write them on the tablet of your heart."
—Proverbs 3:3

What Is Needed: Bible and a copy of a house plan or diagram, picture of a tabernacle if one is available

Making It Real
(*Show the children a copy of a house plan.*) In this house, the designer planned each room carefully and laid it out with its purpose in mind. Did you know that God created His own house plans? God created house plans and called for Moses to build His house, which became known as "the tabernacle." That word means "tent"—or we could think of it as a house. *(Show a picture of a tabernacle. There are several online sources for pictures—photos of a replica are at*

http://www.bibleplaces.com/tabernacle.htm) The tabernacle would be the place where God's Spirit would live on earth during Old Testament times. God told Moses exactly how to build the tabernacle. He gave Moses every measurement and told him how to build everything in it. God even told Moses the color of the curtains. (See Exodus 25–31.) Moses was faithful to follow the instructions that God gave him, down to every little detail.

Moses built the tabernacle because he wanted to follow what God expected him to do. He wanted to obey God because he loved and honored God. This is called *being faithful*. Moses showed he was faithful to God by building the tabernacle according to God's plans.

God wants us to be faithful too. God wants us to follow faithfully the plans and instructions He has given us in the Bible. The Bible is the plan book God has given us to live by.

Prayer

God, help us to be faithful and to follow Your instructions in the Bible.

Making It Stick

Discuss the following question: What does it mean to be faithful?

Read the following verses together. Have children share ideas for how they can be faithful to apply the truths in the verses to the way they live:

- 2 Corinthians 5:7—Faith
- Luke 10:27—Love
- Micah 6:8—Just and merciful actions
- Galatians 5:22–23—Fruit of the Spirit
- Acts 1:8—Missions
- Proverbs 3:3—Remembrance

Making It Personal

Memorize Proverbs 3:3. What does this Scripture verse mean?

Write the verses under Making It Stick on small pieces of paper. Attach them to a string to create a Scripture memory necklace. Wear your necklace to remind you to be faithful to God's Word.

Making It Home

Write down the name of each fruit of the Spirit, as found in Galatians 5:22–23, on an individual slip of paper. Put the slips of paper in a basket on the dinner table. Each time the family sits down for dinner, have a family member take a slip and tell how he or she has lived or will live out that trait for that particular day.

End each dinner this week by repeating Proverbs 3:3 aloud. Discuss how applying the words of the Bible to the way we live shows we are being faithful to God.

David

Missional Message: God will give us strength and courage when we need it.

Missional Challenge:
"'The LORD who delivered me from the paw of the lion and the paw of the bear will deliver me from the hand of this Philistine.' Saul said to David, 'Go, and the LORD be with you.'"
—1 Samuel 17:37

What Is Needed: Bible

Making It Real
Let me see how strong you are. Make a muscle. (*Demonstrate by flexing your biceps whenever you say gigantic giant.*) Wow! You all are very strong. The Bible tells us a story about a strong giant named Goliath in 1 Samuel 17. Every time I say, "Goliath, the gigantic giant," I want you to flex your arm muscles.

(*The following story is a paraphrase of 1 Samuel 17.*) The story goes like this: Years before King David became a king, he was a shepherd boy. His people, the Israelites, were in a battle against the Philistines. Here is where Goliath, the gigantic giant, comes in. The Philistines had Goliath, the gigantic giant, fighting for them. Goliath, the gigantic giant, told the Israelites to send one of their men to fight him. Goliath, the gigantic giant, made a challenge: "If you kill me, you have won the battle, and we become your servants. However, if I kill your man, the Philistines have won and you become our servants." The king of the Israelites and his people were terrified and afraid to fight Goliath, the gigantic giant.

However, David, the youngest of eight brothers, said that he would go and fight Goliath, the gigantic giant. None of David's brothers or the Israelites took David seriously. Even the king said there was no way that a boy could fight Goliath, the gigantic giant. You see, the king knew how gigantic the giant was and how little David was. However, David told the king, "The Lord who delivered me from the paw of the lion and the paw of the bear will deliver me from Goliath, the gigantic giant." So the king gave David his own battle clothes and sent him to fight Goliath, the gigantic giant.

Amazingly, David killed Goliath, the gigantic giant, with a stone and the Philistines ran away. The Israelites were very happy with David.

This story is not about how God made David strong with muscles. (*Show muscles again to illustrate.*) It really is a story about how God gave David what was needed to win the battle.

Prayer

God, thank You for always giving us what we need, even in hard situations.

Making It Stick

(*Initiate discussion with the following questions.*) Think of a time when you relied on God for courage and strength. What were those times? How did you respond? What did you do?

Here are some examples of circumstances that people we call "missionaries" come in contact with every day. Think of the many ways that God helps missionaries be courageous and strong in these situations.

- Moving to a place where you have to make new friends.
- Moving to a place where you have to learn a new language.
- Living in a place where you do not have a car, so you have to walk everywhere.
- Moving to a place where some people do not want you in their community.

Making It Personal

Memorize 1 Samuel 17:37. Personalize the words in this verse, using your own experiences or circumstances during which God has already delivered and protected you and continues to protect you.

Give thanks to God that you can rely on Him for courage and strength.

Making It Home

Cut out pictures from old magazines or use poster board and markers to create a collage or a poster together that displays all of the times in the life of your family when God has given family members courage and/or strength. Celebrate how God has protected and helped you.

Esther

Missional Message: God gives us peace.

Missional Challenge:
"Peace I leave with you; my peace I give you. I do not give to you as the world gives. Do not let your hearts be troubled and do not be afraid."
—John 14:27

What Is Needed: Bible

Making It Real

Have you ever been in the situation where you had to stand up for what was right even when it was hard?

There is a story in the Bible about a girl named Esther. Esther was a young woman. She was chosen by the king in the land where she lived to be his wife. You see, Esther lived in a land where most of the people did not believe in the one true God, in whom the Israelites, her people, believed. The king was unaware that Esther believed in God.

She kept that a secret from him, as instructed by a close relative.

One of the king's advisors hated the Israelites, so he encouraged the king to ask for all Israelites to be killed. Esther was faced with a serious problem. She could stay quiet and save herself, or she could tell the king and possibly be killed herself for approaching the king uninvited or simply for being an Israelite.

Esther made the right decision. She stood up to the king and asked him not to let the Israelites be killed. The king heard her and withdrew the plans to kill her people.

At times in our lives, God asks us to do things that are difficult. Standing up to a bully or telling on someone when you know that they have done something wrong can be very hard. (*Read John 14:27.*) God gives us peace when we have reason to be troubled or afraid. When we think that we need to stand up for someone or for what we know is right, we need to seek God for guidance and rely on His peace.

Prayer

God, thank You for being with us always and everywhere. Help us not to worry in hard situations, but to stand up for what You have taught us.

Making It Stick

Here are a few difficult situations in which boys and girls may find themselves. Present the following and discuss the ways that God would want us to respond.

- Someone is talking bad about someone else.
- You realize that a friend has lied to you about something.
- A classmate is giving out the answers to the next math test.
- You see someone steal a pencil.
- You accidentally break someone else's toy.
- Someone is making fun of Christians.

Making It Personal

Memorize John 14:27.

Write a prayer to God telling Him about a hard situation that you are going through. Ask Him to help you to know what to do and to guide you to make good decisions.

Making It Home

Parents, share with your children a difficult situation that God brought you through and how He gave you peace.

Isaiah

Missional Message: God wants us to tell other people about Him.

Missional Challenge:
"'You are my witnesses,' declares the LORD, 'and my servant whom I have chosen, so that you may know and believe me and understand that I am he. Before me no god was formed, nor will there be one after me.'"
—Isaiah 43:10

What Is Needed: Megaphone, Bible

Making It Real
(Using the megaphone, make the following announcement.)
   People of _____ *(Insert community name)*, I have come to tell you about the coming of the Lord. Stop doing bad things and follow God. God loves you!
   (Put the megaphone down and continue.) In the Old Testament

of the Bible, we are introduced to prophets. Prophets were people whom God spoke through to speak to others on His behalf. God used prophets to warn people that they must stop doing bad things or God would punish them. Prophets also told about the coming of Jesus. In the Book of Isaiah in the Bible, we hear the story of the prophet Isaiah. God told Isaiah things that He wanted Isaiah to tell the kings of his time.

Isaiah told several kings how God was going to punish their nation because they had turned away from God and were following their own ways instead of God's ways. Isaiah did not bring all bad news, though. He also told the good news of the coming of Jesus. He told how God would come to earth as a man and save the people. Jesus is that One that Isaiah promised.

(Read Isaiah 43:10.) This verse tells us that God was talking to the people and letting them know that they needed to tell others that He is the one true God.

Today, God wants us to be messengers for God, to tell others about Jesus.

Prayer
God, thank You for allowing us to tell other people about You.

Making It Stick
Have children develop one or more skits that portray them telling others about God.

Making It Personal
Memorize Isaiah 43:10.

Have you recently told someone you know about Jesus? What did you say. Write down what you would share about Jesus with a friend. Then talk about the things you wrote down with a friend.

Making It Home
Discuss how your family can tell others the good news. Talk about what it means to be a prophet in today's world.

Jesus— Christmas

11

Missional Message: God sent Jesus to give us life.

Missional Challenge:
"For I have come down from heaven not to do my will but to do the will of him who sent me.... For my Father's will is that everyone who looks to the Son and believes in him shall have eternal life, and I will raise him up at the last day."
—John 6:38, 40

What Is Needed: Bible, something to symbolize a birthday such as a candle, banner, or birthday balloon, construction paper, markers or pencils, and birthday cake or cupcakes if you think the time is appropriate

Making It Real
(Show the children the birthday item.)
What does this remind you of? *(Anticipated answer: birthday)* Let's sing happy birthday to Jesus.

Birthdays are very special. A birthday is the day we celebrate every year to remember the day that we were born. We use this day to count how many years it has been since we were born. On the day of your birth, people celebrated you coming to the earth. (*Share a story of how happy you were when your child or a relative's or friend's child was born.*)

Jesus's birthday was special, because it was God's Son coming to earth. We know that Joseph and Mary celebrated the birth of Jesus. We celebrate Jesus's birthday every year at Christmas.

Christmas reminds us that God sent Jesus to us. In the Book of John 6:38 and 40, Jesus tells us that He came from heaven to earth to follow God. God sent Jesus to earth to teach us how to live and to give us life.

Christmas is more that just a birthday celebration for Jesus. It is a celebration of God sending Jesus to earth because of His love for us. It is a celebration of Jesus making a way for us to have life with God in heaven.

This year at Christmas, celebrate Jesus.

Prayer
God, thank You for sending Jesus to us.

Making It Stick
Cut out a birthday candle shape from construction paper for each child. On one side, have children write why they are happy that Jesus was born. On the other side, have them write ways they can share the joy of Jesus with others at Christmas. Have the children share their ideas with one another.

Making It Personal
Read John 10:10; John 3:16; and John 6:40. Write down what these verses are saying about life with God. How do we have life with God?

Making It Home
This year, use colorful paper, markers, and other art supplies to make Scripture notes that witness to the reason for Christmas. Insert these

notes in Christmas cards or attach them to gifts. For example, write, "Jesus gives life." (John 10:10) or "You are loved." (John 3:16). As a family, create your own notes of encouragement based on Scripture verses, and provide the references. Talk together about what the Scriptures mean.

Disciples

Missional Message: God wants us to follow Jesus.

Missional Challenge:
"Whoever serves me must follow me; and where I am, my servant also will be. My Father will honor the one who serves me."
—John 12:26

What Is Needed: Bible, paper, and pencils, poster board or dry wipe board.

Making It Real
Have you ever played "follow the leader"? Let's practice. (*Lead the children to pat their heads, raise their hands above their heads, and lastly, to smile.*) We learn in the Bible that Jesus asked people to follow Him. As people followed Him, He taught them by telling stories about God's kingdom and preaching on how they should live.

Jesus asked 12 men to follow Him daily. The Bible calls those men *disciples*, which means "follower." They were very close to Jesus and followed Him everywhere. They witnessed Jesus healing and performing miracles. Jesus taught them what to teach, He showed them where to go, and He gave them the power to do many of the things that He could do.

Before Jesus went to heaven, He told His disciples to go and make followers of all people and nations. He wanted the disciples to baptize them and teach them all that He had taught them. The disciples followed Jesus (Matthew 28:18–20).

Today, Jesus wants all believers to be His disciples. He wants us to be followers of Him, Christ followers. He wants us to follow His teaching and then to take what we learn to teach others.

(*Read John 12:26.*) These are Jesus's words to us. They are very serious words, and Jesus is serious about wanting us to be His followers. He wants us to give up what we want and to focus on following Him.

Prayer
God, help us to follow You as your disciples.

Making It Stick
(*Draw a picture of a simple sailboat on the poster or on a dry wipe board. Have the children copy your drawing.*) Just as you copied my drawing, Jesus wants you to copy Him.

Below their drawing, have the children list some ways that they can follow Jesus.

Making It Personal
Memorize John 12:26.

Make two columns on a piece of paper. In the first column, write some of the things that Jesus did, such as His miracles. In the second column, write how you can follow Him.

Making It Home
Parents, share with your children how you strive to follow Jesus. Tell them a personal story about a time when you had to give up something to follow Jesus. As a family, discuss ways that you can follow Jesus.

Jesus— Easter

Missional Message: Jesus Christ died for us.

Missional Challenge:
"But God demonstrates his own love for us in this: While we were still sinners, Christ died for us."
—Romans 5:8

What Is Needed: Bible and world globe

Making It Real
(*Show the children the globe.*)

This globe shows every country on earth. In each country, there are people with languages, customs, and beliefs that are probably different from yours. The Bible says that God loved the world—every person—so much that He sent His Son, Jesus, to earth (John 3:16). As we read the Bible, we learn about Jesus's birth, life, death, and coming back to life.

God sent Jesus to earth for a very special reason. Jesus was God's only Son. He came to earth so that He could be human like us. But there is one thing that Jesus did not do that we do. He did not sin. Jesus was the only sinless man to ever live. Sins are the things people do that are against what God wants us to do. Not only does sin displease God, but it separates each of us from God (Romans 6:23).

Jesus provided a way for us to know God. He wanted us to be able to talk to God without our sin getting in the way. Remember, Jesus never sinned. So Jesus was the one person in the world who could give His life so that everyone would have the opportunity to get to know God (Romans 4:25).

Jesus gave His life by dying for us on a cross, to take away our sins. Yes, Jesus died. But three days later, God brought Him back to life. Because Jesus died and came back to life, we have a way for us to ask God for forgiveness for our sin. We still sin, but God can forgive us because of Jesus (Acts 2:29–38).

Prayer
God, thank You for sending Jesus to provide a way for us to know You.

Making It Stick
Discuss how sins are those things that displease God. Let children think of and say some sins. Write the sins on a board. Discuss how God has provided a way for us to receive forgiveness of sins by believing in Jesus and praying to God, asking for forgiveness. Say a simple model prayer asking for forgiveness of sins so that the children understand how to ask God to forgive them for things they do that God doesn't want us to do.

Making It Personal
Memorize Romans 5:8.

This week, begin your prayertime by telling your sins to God and asking for forgiveness.

Making It Home
Parents, share with your children what Jesus means to you. Share how you, too, ask forgiveness for your sins.

Paul

Missional Message: God uses people to tell about Jesus and to start churches.

Missional Challenge:
"I have been crucified with Christ and I no longer live, but Christ lives in me. The life I live in the body, I live by faith in the Son of God, who loved me and gave himself for me."
—Galatians 2:20

What Is Needed: Bible and adventure gear, such as hiking boots and life jackets

Making It Real

(Show children some adventure gear.) Today, we hear stories about extreme adventurers sailing across the ocean, climbing mountains, and doing many other extreme activities. The Bible tells us about a great adventurer named Paul. Even though he did not set out to be an adventurer, following God took Paul on a great adventure.

Before Paul knew Jesus, he wanted to kill the people that believed in Jesus (Acts 8:1–3; 9:1–2). Once Paul met Jesus, his life forever changed. Paul gave up his life to follow Jesus and to start churches. Paul's adventures included traveling extensively, being thrown into prison, surviving three shipwrecks, being beaten and stoned, and finding himself in the middle of many church conflicts.

Paul took advantage of every opportunity that he had to share Jesus, even some dangerous ones. When he was called to testify in front of King Agrippa, he preached about Jesus the Christ, the Son of God (Acts 26). When he was in prison, he preached to the guards and continued to write letters to the church leaders encouraging them to live for God.

(Read Galatians 2:20.) Paul is saying that he has given up everything to preach to others about Jesus.

I pray that each of us will follow the example of Paul and want to tell about Jesus so badly that nothing can stop us.

Prayer
God, thank You for giving us Paul as an example for us to live by.

Making It Stick
Read 2 Corinthians 11:23–28. After each time that Paul lists a hardship he has endured for Jesus the Christ, tell the children to say, "I live for Christ." If you have extra time, you could lead the children to act out some of the experiences that Paul went through.

Making It Personal
Memorize Galatians 2:20. This memory verse may be a little difficult to understand. Paul said that he gave up who he used to be so that he could be more like Jesus the Christ and that Jesus the Christ led him in every part of his life.

Make a drawing or comic strip that illustrates Paul's adventures.

Making It Home
As a family, read Acts 26. Discuss how Paul gave evidence for the truth of Jesus's death and resurrection, in front of King Agrippa. What can we learn from the way Paul answered Agrippa's questions?

Antioch

Missional Message: God's message of good news is for everyone.

Missional Challenge:
"Some of them, however, men from Cyprus and Cyrene, went to Antioch and began to speak to Greeks also, telling them the good news about the Lord Jesus. The Lord's hand was with them, and a great number of people believed and turned to the Lord."
—Acts 11:20–21

What Is Needed: Bible and pictures depicting people from different religious backgrounds

Making It Real
(*Show pictures of people from different religious backgrounds. You can find pictures online at wikipedia.com. Also check travel magazines, encyclopedias, and social studies textbooks.*) The people in these

pictures represent people from many places in the world, who have not yet heard the good news about Jesus. God wants us to go to all people to tell them about Jesus.

Some people may think that the good news of Jesus is just for certain people who look like them and act like them. Some people in the first churches thought that too. The Jewish people were the ones in the Old Testament whom God had worked through. The disciples were Jewish. At first, the disciples preached only to others who were also Jewish. However, God led some of the disciples to travel to Antioch, a town which was in the place we now call Turkey. The disciples were to tell the *Gentiles*, a word that means "people who are not Jewish," about Jesus. *(If you have a world globe or map, point out where Turkey is.)* The Gentiles at that time were the people known as "the Greeks," or people who lived within the Roman Empire and who were not Jewish.

We read in Acts 11:20–21 that God's Spirit came upon the disciples, and that they began telling the Gentiles about the good news of Jesus. The Gentiles accepted the good news and followed God. However, we see that some of the Jewish believers soon tried to make the Gentiles follow their Jewish rules (Acts 15:1).

Basically, what happened is that the first of the Jewish-Christians wanted to keep the good news of Jesus for themselves, and then they wanted to impose their own rules and regulations on the new believers. Despite all of this, more and more Greeks became believers and followers of Jesus because God's Spirit was with them.

The Bible says that the name *Christian* was first given to the disciples in the town of Antioch.

Prayer
God, help us to remember that the good news of Jesus is for everyone. Give us the courage to tell the good news to everyone.

Making It Stick
Discuss these questions: Why do you think the Jewish people wanted to keep Jesus for themselves and not to share Him with others? Do you think that attitude is true with some Christians today? What keeps us

from telling people that are different from us about Jesus?

Review the pictures from Making It Real. Ask the children if they think it would be easy or hard to tell the persons in the pictures about Jesus. Discuss the reasoning behind their apprehensions.

Making It Personal
Memorize Acts 11:20–21.

Are you afraid to tell the good news of Jesus to some people? Ask God to give you courage and opportunity to tell others about Him.

Making It Home
Discuss with your family these questions: Do we have friends who are not Christians? How can we build friendships with non-Christians?

Pray that God will provide opportunities for your family to meet and befriend people who are not Christians. Ask God to give you ways to share your love and faith in Jesus Christ with others from different cultural and religious or nonreligious backgrounds.

Holy Spirit

Missional Message: God gives believers the Holy Spirit.

Missional Challenge:
"Peter replied, 'Repent and be baptized, every one of you, in the name of Jesus Christ for the forgiveness of your sins. And you will receive the gift of the Holy Spirit.'"
—Acts 2:38

What Is Needed: Bible and gift box or bag

Making It Real
(*Show the children the gift box or bag.*)

Have you ever seen something like this? What is it? How many of you like getting gifts? I love getting and giving gifts.

God has given us many things as gifts. He especially, gave us Jesus. Then when Jesus left the earth, God sent the Holy Spirit to be with us.

What can we learn in the Bible about the Holy Spirit? In Genesis 1:2, we learn that the Holy Spirit was with God when He created the world. We see in the Old Testament that the Spirit was working at different times among the people of God. In the New Testament, Jesus talked about the Holy Spirit being with Him and His disciples.

After Jesus died and came back to life but before He went to heaven, He went to His disciples and told them to receive the Holy Spirit (John 20:22). Jesus sent the Holy Spirit to those who believed in Him, and the Holy Spirit also comes to help Christ followers today. The Bible says, *"Repent and be baptized, every one of you, in the name of Jesus Christ for the forgiveness of your sins. And you will receive the gift of the Holy Spirit"* (Acts 2:38). We receive the Holy Spirit when we believe in Jesus and follow Him.

The Holy Spirit helps us do lots of things. The Holy Spirit counsels us to do the things that God wants us to do. The Holy Spirit helps us to understand the Bible. The Holy Spirit gives us God's power to tell the good news. The Holy Spirit gives us joy to share with others. The Holy Spirit lets us know when we have sinned against God (John 14:26; Acts 1:8; Romans 14:17; 1 Thessalonians 1:6; John 16:8).

Prayer
God, thank You for giving us the Holy Spirit.

Making It Stick
Explain that, at first, learning about the Holy Spirit may seem a little strange, but help the children think of the Holy Spirit as a gift that God has given to us to help us through life. God does this because He loves us. Read the following verses to teach about the Holy Spirit:

- Genesis 1:2
- Acts 1:8
- Acts 4:31
- Galatians 5:22
- John 14:16–17
- John 14:26
- Acts 9:31
- Romans 14:17

- Romans 5:3–5
- Romans 8:26–27

Making It Personal
Memorize John 14:26.

Take time to read the Bible this week. Before you begin to read, pray and ask the Holy Spirit to help you understand what you are reading.

Making It Home
Share with your children how the Holy Spirit has been a part of your life. Pray together, asking the Holy Spirit to guide your family's learning experiences in the Bible and sharing of God's Word.

Heaven

Missional Message: God wants us to live with Him in heaven.

Missional Challenge:
"In my Father's house are many rooms; if it were not so, I would have told you. I am going there to prepare a place for you. And if I go and prepare a place for you, I will come back and take you to be with me that you also may be where I am."
—John 14:2–3

What Is Needed: Bible, paper, and pencils

Making It Real

Where is your favorite place to visit? (*Let the children share.*)

Would you believe that I know a place that is much better than any of those places? The place is heaven. Heaven is the most wonderful place. God has created heaven as a place for us to live with Him.

Before Jesus went to heaven, He said that He would come back to earth one day and take those who believe and follow Him to heaven to live with Him. John 14:2–3 says this: (*Read the verses.*) To those believers who die before He returns, He promises that they will go to heaven to be with Him.

The Bible tells us about heaven. We learn that it is where God lives and the place from where He rules. We learn that it is a place that God has prepared for His people. We know there are angels, streets of gold, places to stay, no hunger, and no sadness (Revelation 7:16–17; 21:1–27). We will be with Jesus when we go to heaven and we will worship Him.

Prayer
God, thank You for making heaven for us to live in forever and where we will worship You.

Making It Stick
(*Read Luke 8:1.*) Why do you think Jesus preached about the kingdom of God?

Lead children to offer some answers, making sure to emphasize these points: Jesus wants people to believe in Him, confess their sins, and to follow Him, so that they can live with the Holy Spirit on earth and live with God and Jesus in heaven.

Have children write a letter that thanks God for making a place for us to live forever. Or, have them draw a picture of what they think heaven is like. Underneath it write, "Thank You, God, for heaven."

Making It Personal
Memorize John 14:2–3.

Read John 14:2–3 again and then read John 3:16. Think about how much Jesus loves you that He would give His life so that we could live forever in heaven. Thank God for the love and care that He has given to us.

Making It Home

Research the word *heaven* in the Bible. Check crosswalk.com or a Bible dictionary if you need some help in defining what the word means. You might also do a key word search at biblegateway.com which can locate verses with the word *heaven* in them. Select and read some of the identified verses with your family. Make a list of all the characteristics of heaven that you find.

11 Foundations of Missional Living

Active Compassion

18

Missional Message: God wants us to live lives of compassion.

Missional Challenge:
"Therefore, as God's chosen people, holy and dearly loved, clothe yourselves with compassion, kindness, humility, gentleness and patience."
—Colossians 3:12

What Is Needed: Bible, pictures from magazines or newspapers that display active compassion, and a jacket labeled with the word compassion

Making It Real
What is compassion? When you have compassion, you feel that you want to do something to help others. Here are some examples of compassion. (*Show three to four pictures of compassion being demonstrated: for example, someone being fed, someone being cared for, someone being prayed for.*)

The Bible says in Colossians 3:12 that we should be full of compassion. (*Read the verse from the Bible.*) It says to "clothe yourselves" with compassion. (*Put on a jacket that you have labeled with a sign that says "compassion" on the front and/or back of it.*) Is this want Jesus was saying?

God is saying, let people see compassion coming from what you do, not really from what you wear. God wants Christians to be seen by others as being compassionate people. As a Christian, you are representing to other people what it means to be a follower of Jesus.

Let's look at examples of Jesus showing His compassion so that we can follow Him:
- (*Read Mark 6:34.*) He had compassion on people who did not know about God, so He taught them.
- (*Read Matthew 14:14.*) Jesus had compassion for the sick, so He healed them.
- (*Read Matthew 15:32.*) He had compassion for the hungry, so He fed them.

Do you notice something about all three of these examples? In every example when Jesus had compassion, He did something about it. Jesus demonstrated active compassion. He did not just feel sorry for the people, but He did something to help.

Each day we are given opportunities to show compassion to others. Pray that when you see people in need, you will respond, just like Jesus did—with active compassion.

Prayer
God, help us to show compassion to others just like Jesus did.

Making It Stick
Let children act out the scenarios below. After each dramatization, have the child say how they would show active compassion.
- A family's home burns down.
- Someone at your school does not have food at home.
- Someone gets sick on the school bus.

Making It Personal
Memorize Colossian 3:12.

What is a need in your community? What can you do about it? Pray that God will provide an opportunity for you to show active compassion.

Making It Home
Discuss how your family can respond to needs in your community with active compassion. Use these sites to learn how your family can be advocates for compassion in your communities: www.worldvision.org or www.bread.org. Or perhaps you know of a local organization that works with people who are needy in some way. Call to see if you can volunteer as a family in any number of ways for those organizations.

Mission Action

Missional Message: God can use children to do missions.

Missional Challenge:
"Dear children, let us not love with words or tongue but with actions and in truth."
—1 John 3:18

What Is Needed: Bible, dry wipe board, four posters for illustration, and stickers, paper, and markers for the newsletter

Making It Real
(*Write the following phrases on posters or on the dry wipe board:* Acts of Kindness, Giving to Others, Praying for Others, *and* Caring for Others. *Talk about each point separately, describing examples of each mission action. You may use mission action stories from your own church, community, or experience in the place of the following examples.*)

Raise your hand if you can do missions. What does it mean when we say we "do missions?" *(Encourage some answers and write them on the board.)*

There are many ways to "do missions" (Tell some of your churches stories). Yes, you can do missions! Each one of you can do missions. Let's look at some examples:

- *Acts of Kindness:* Show others the love of Jesus by doing random acts to show kindness. One children's group in Florida provided at their town fair a baby-changing station for mothers with young children. They distributed free water, provided information about becoming a Christian, and invited people to their church.
- *Giving to Others:* To persons living in poverty, give food, clothing, shelter, transportation, or resource needs they might have. One girls' group in Alabama bought and gave school supplies to a ministry that tutors children in the inner city.
- *Praying for Others:* Pray for the people you know of who have spiritual, mental, emotional, or physical needs. You can pray for others at any time. You do not even have to be with the persons to pray for them. One family in Texas makes a point to pray for the people in their church weekly. You can also research different people groups so that you know how to pray for those people.
- *Caring for Others:* You can visit people who are sick or alone. A group in California goes every month to a nearby nursing home to cheer up the elderly people who live there.

I am sure that you can think of many other ways to minister to others. An adult can help you to do any of your mission action projects.

Acts of kindness, giving to others, praying for others, and caring for others are ways to show God's love. First John 3:18 says, *"Dear children, let us not love with words or tongue but with actions and in truth."*

We are following God when we love others through mission action.

Prayer
God, thank You for using us to do missions to share Your love.

Making It Stick
Visit www.childrensmissions.com. Look to see how children's groups are ministering to others. Print some of the stories and share them with the children. Have them create and implement a mission action project.

Making It Personal
Memorize 1 John 3:18.

Think about a mission action project that you want to do. Write out a plan. Share your plan with an adult, so the adult can provide guidance for you. Implement your plan.

Making It Home
Talk about different needs in your community. As a family, drive around your community and city to assess the needs. Pray about how your family can start ministering together in your community or city. On Saturday, prayerwalk, as a family, an area where you have noticed a need.

Extra Missional Opportunities
Get your group involved in Children's Ministry Day™ (www.childrensmissions.com).

Following Jesus

Missional Message: God shows me how to become a Christian.

Missional Challenge:
"Greater love has no one than this, that he lay down his life for his friends."
—John 15:13

What Is Needed: Picture of best friend, Bible

Making It Real
(Show a picture of your best friend and tell the children about the friendship you have with your best friend.)

God created each of us with the desire for us to know Him. God wants to be our Friend. However, as is the case with many friendships, something hurt the friendship. That something is sin. Sin separates us from God's friendship and love. An example of a sin is disobeying what the Bible tells us to do.

The Bible says that everyone has sinned (Romans 3:23). In fact, sin separates us from a friendship with God.

Despite our sin, God loved us so very much that He sent His Son, Jesus, to save us from our sins. Since Jesus lived a sinless life on earth, He was able to make a way for our sins to be forgiven. Jesus gave Himself, by dying for our sins, so that we might know God as our friend.

God wants us to believe that Jesus came to earth, lived a sinless life, and died to forgive us of our sins. Then God wants us to commit our lives to following Jesus. This is a process that many people call *being saved,* because God is saving us from our sins and providing us with a way to know Him.

So how are you saved? The Bible says in Romans 10:9, *"That if you confess with your mouth, 'Jesus is Lord,' and believe in your heart that God raised him from the dead, you will be saved."*

All you have to do is believe and ask Jesus to save you.

Prayer

God, thank You for loving us so much that You have provided a way for us to know You as our Friend.

Making It Stick

Have the children write the following verses or draw pictures that illustrate the verses. Lead the children to share in their own words what the verses mean. Help them to understand the meaning of words they might not know, such as *wages* and *confess.*

- "For all have sinned and fall short of the glory of God" *(Romans 3:23).*
- "But God demonstrates his own love for us in this: While we were still sinners, Christ died for us" *(Romans 5:8).*
- "For the wages of sin is death, but the gift of God is eternal life in Christ Jesus our Lord" *(Romans 6:23).*
- "If we confess our sins, he is faithful and just and will forgive us our sins and purify us from all unrighteousness" *(1 John 1:9).*

- *"That if you confess with your mouth, 'Jesus is Lord,' and believe in your heart that God raised him from the dead, you will be saved" (Romans 10:9).*

If a child is interested in learning more or in making a personal decision to follow Christ, counsel with the child one-on-one.

Making It Personal
Memorize Romans 10:9.

Write a letter to God, thanking Him for sending Jesus. Share that letter with a friend.

Making It Home
Have each family member share about when he or she chose to follow Christ.

21 Knowing God

Missional Message: God wants us to seek Him through His Word and prayer.

Missional Challenge: *"'You will seek me and find me when you seek me with all your heart. I will be found by you,' declares the LORD."*
—Jeremiah 29:13–14a

What Is Needed: Bible, paper for journal or photocopy page 74, pencils, brads or ties, and construction paper for covers

Making It Real

Raise your hand if you have friends. Can anyone tell me what a friend is? What does the word *friendship* means to you? (*Let children share.*)

To become friends with someone, you have to get to know them. You get to know people as friends by spending time with them and talking with them. It is the same with God.

Listen to what the Bible says about God wanting to be close to us. (*Read Jeremiah 29:13–14*a, *as in the Missional Challenge above.*) This means that we can know God. We know God by seeking after Him. When making friends with people, you have to spend time with them to get to know them, you have to spend time with God to get to know Him. Let's talk about two ways we can spend time with God.

One way is to take time to read and learn the Bible. The Bible is God's Word. It is a record of what God has told the world about Himself. The Bible is our guidebook to all things about God! Everything we need to know about God is in the Bible. God wants us to read and study the Bible so that we will know more about Him.

The second way to know God is to take time to pray. God wants us to talk to Him by praying. You can talk to God about anything and everything. He wants to hear the good, the bad, the silly, and the sad. Everything! God already knows your thoughts—but as the good friend that He is, He wants you to be honest with Him.

Prayer
God, thank You for letting us know You through the Bible and through prayer.

Making It Stick
Have the children create a one-week journal. They can create their own or you can photocopy page 74 for them. Children can decorate construction-paper covers and attach with brads or yarn ties, or simply staple together. Lead children to complete one of their journal pages using Jeremiah 29:13–14*a*.

Making It Personal
Memorize Jeremiah 29:13–14*a*.

Write in your journal each day this week, learning about a different Scripture verse. Afterwards, spend time praying.

Making It Home
Have each family member journal this week. At the end of the week, ask everyone to share some of the things that Bible study and prayer taught them about God.

Knowing God

My Knowing God Journal

My name is: _____

The Scripture I read today was _____

This verse means _____

_____

_____

_____

I can apply this verse to my life by _____

_____

_____

_____

My prayer today is _____

_____

_____

_____

_____

_____

22

Loving God

Missional Message: God wants me to love Him.

Missional Challenge:
"He answered: 'Love the Lord your God with all your heart and with all your soul and with all your strength and with all your mind'; and 'Love your neighbor as yourself.'"
—Luke 10:27

What Is Needed: Bible, a secular love song to sing and/or a CD player with CD of the song, four index cards per child, and pencils and/or markers

Making It Real
(Start the lesson by singing or playing on a CD player a popular secular song that you know about love: for example "What the World Needs Now")

There are many songs about love. Can you think of more? *(Children may name songs such as "Jesus Loves Me.")*

I have a question about love for you to think about. How do you love God? The Bible tells us exactly how we are to love God in the Bible. The book of Luke in the New Testament tells us of a time a person asked Jesus what he must do to have eternal life. Jesus responded by asking the man to tell Him what the Bible said.

The man responded with our verse for today: *"'Love the Lord your God with all your heart and with all your soul and with all your strength and with all your mind'; and, 'Love your neighbor as yourself.'"*

Jesus told the man his answer was right.

That passage from the Bible tells me how I need to love the Lord:
- Love the Lord my God with all my heart. My heart represents my emotions.
- Love God with all my soul. Wow! My soul is the inner spiritual part of me. The soul is the very deepest part of who humans are.
- Love God with all my mind. My mind represents all my thoughts.
- Love God with all my strength. God even wants me to love Him with my muscles!

Hey, wait a minute! I am starting to see something: God wants me to love Him with all that I am—with everything I am, do, and say. God wants us all to love Him in that way.

Prayer
God, help me to love You with all that I am. Help me to love other people the way that You love them.

Making It Stick
Have the children write on index cards the following words:
- My Emotions
- My Soul
- My Thoughts
- My Muscles

Underneath each word, have the children write how they can love God with that aspect of themselves.

Making It Personal
Memorize Luke 10:27.

Draw a picture for God, showing how you love Him.

Making It Home
As a family, each of you can write a love letter to God telling of the ways you love Him. Let each person share his or her letter with the other family members. Have a family prayertime telling God how much He is loved by everyone in your family.

Loving Others
23

Missional Message: God wants me to love others.

Missional Challenge:
"My command is this: Love each other as I have loved you."
—John 15:12

What Is Needed: Bible and video camera, if available

Making It Real

Not so long ago, there used to be a show on television called *Mister Rogers' Neighborhood*. Raise your hand if you have seen it. *(The old shows may still be on television in some places.)* Every day the first thing Mister Rogers did was to sing a song that invited you into his neighborhood. The song goes like this: "It's a beautiful day in the neighborhood.... Please, won't you be my neighbor?"

Mister Rogers was a minister, in real life which means he once had a job similar to our pastor *(name)*'s. He dedicated his life to children by creating a television show that taught children how to be kind and loving towards the people they saw every day—teachers, friends, family, even the people next door, who we think of as "neighbors." Mister Rogers knew the Bible tells us to love our neighbors as we love ourselves (Leviticus 19:18; Luke 10:27). Did you know that Jesus teaches us that everyone is our neighbor?

(Read John 15:12.) These are Jesus's words. He says that God wants us to love others. He wants us to love other people like He loves us. Remember that God loves us so much that He gave us Jesus. That shows God's love for us.

We can love other people by how we live and what we say. *(Let the children respond to the following questions. Be prepared to guide them with suggestions.)*

- How can we show others God's love?
- What are words you can say to show others you love them?
- What actions can we take to show others that we love them?

Prayer
God, thank You for showing us how to love others. Help us to love You and to love other people.

Making It Stick
Have the children create a short TV sketch or skit that teaches children how to love others. If you have more than five children, divide them into small groups for creating the sketch. If you have a video camera, film each group's sketch as they perform, and then watch the skits together.

Making It Personal
Memorize John 15:12.

Make a list of the people whom you consider hard to love. Pray that God will help you to love these people as He does. This week, do your best to be kind to these people to show them that you care for them.

Making It Home
If you have a video camera, make a family video that teaches about loving others. Invite other families over to have a family game night and to preview your homemade video.

If you have a Web site or blog, post your video there for families and friends to view. If you are adept at using Godtube, consider putting it there. (When using public Web sites, keep in mind your family's safety and limit the personal information you provide—but there is no doubt that these outlets provide wide coverage for a positive message.)

My Purpose

Missional Message: God has a plan and purpose for my life.

Missional Challenge:
"For you created my inmost being; you knit me together in my mother's womb. I praise you because I am fearfully and wonderfully made."
—Psalm 139:13–14a

What Is Needed: Bible, paper, markers or pencils; sculpture, needlework, quilt, and/or other hand-crafted item to use as an illustration

Making It Real
(*Show a sample of a sculpture or something that has been crafted by hand.*)

The person who made this item spent lots of time making it. Have you ever made something special, maybe as a gift for your mother or father? You take care to make something just the way you want it to be.

Let me share with you what the Bible says in Psalm 139:13–14 about how God made us. (*Read that Scripture.*)

God made each of us when we were inside our mothers. This passage tells us that God created each of us just the way He wanted us to be. Each person is uniquely made by God. He created us with a plan and a purpose for our lives.

Look at your hands. Your hands were created to do lots of things. Think about the things you do with your hands: clap, wave, touch, grab, and make things such as the things I showed you. God created your hands to do all those things and much more. Not only did God create your hands with a purpose in mind but He created every part of you with a purpose in mind. He designed every part of you to use those parts. He gave you to honor Him. God wants us to use all that He has created in us to worship Him and serve Him by ministering to others.

Prayer
God, thank You for creating us for a purpose.

Making It Stick
Have children trace one of their hands. In each finger traced, have them write something special about how God made them. In the palm, write out "I am wonderfully made." Then have the children share their pictures. Take time to point out specific ways that each child was created as a person like no one else to honor and serve God in his or her own special way.

Making It Personal
Memorize Psalm 139:14.

This week, read the verse each night and think about how God has made you for a purpose. List on a sheet of paper the ways that God could use you, and hang the paper where you can see it each day.

Making It Home
Make a family poster with individual handprints. On each handprint, write a way that person can serve God.

My Part

Missional Message: God wants Christ's followers to work together.

Missional Challenge:
"So in Christ we who are many form one body, and each member belongs to all the others. We have different gifts, according to the grace given us."
—Romans 12:5–6a

What Is Needed: Bible, a metal or plastic chain for the illustration, several strips of colorful 2-by-8½-inch paper for each child, and tape or glue sticks

Making It Real

(*Show the children a very strong chain. Pull on the chain to show how strong the chain is.*) This chain is very strong. God wants the church or followers of Christ to be connected, to work together, just like these chain links. When the followers of Christ work together, the work can be done in the best way possible, with strength.

God has provided many passages in the Bible about working together. (*Read Romans 12:4–8.*) In this passage, God is saying the parts of our physical bodies have different functions. He says that the church is like our own bodies in that each person has a different role or job to do. Each follower of Christ in the church has a different job because each person is good at doing something. God wants us all to work together, using the gifts and talents that He has given us to strengthen the church. Working together to build God's church is the work of the church.

When I look around, I see children and adults with lots of different gifts and talents. Every single one of you has something special about you that God created in you. (*Give examples of how you have seen children in the church group strengthen one another by using their unique gifts or talents. Do not use specific names.*) When followers of Christ work together in the church, it makes God happy.

Prayer
God, thank You for giving us an example of how You want us to work together. And help us each to use our gifts and talents to work better together.

Making It Stick
Have the children create a paper-link chain. Have each child write on a 2-by-8½-inch strip of paper the gifts and talents he or she has. Assist children as needed. Children can each complete several strips. When the children have completed their strips, have them combine and interlock their strips with the other children's strips with tape or glue sticks. Make sure the words show on the outside. With the last strip, lock all the strips together to make a circle and hang it in the room.

Describe how, when we all do our parts and work together, we are stronger as a group and can tell more people about Jesus.

Making It Personal
Memorize Romans 12:5–6a.

Write a list of what you think you are good at doing on a 4" x 6" card. Place this list in your Bible. Pray that God will help you use these skills or talents to show and/or tell others about Him. Each time you see the list in your Bible, pray that God will help you use these skills or talents in a way that will strengthen other people.

Making It Home
Make a family chain by holding hands around the dinner table. Discuss how the family supports one another. Also discuss situations in which family members may need help from one another. Talk about the ways that a family can strengthen one another in areas of weakness.

My Time

Missional Message: God cares about the way I spend my time.

Missional Challenge:
"Be very careful, then, how you live—not as unwise but as wise, making the most of every opportunity."
—Ephesians 5:15–16a

What Is Needed: Bible, current calendar, paper with a simple calendar grid preprinted on it for each child to make a calendar page, and markers or pencils

Making It Real

Who can tell me how many months there are in a year? Who knows how many days there are in a year? A place that you can keep up with all the months and days in a year is on a calendar. (*Show the calendar.*) How many of you have a calendar in your home? Most people use calendars to record important dates and appointments so they will remember them in the future.

If your family is like mine, you may have a full day of things to do every day of the week. I am going to give you a few examples of activities, and I want you to raise your hand if I state something that someone in your family does. (*Add activities that you know the children in your group participate in.*)

- Attend music classes.
- Play a sport.
- Take dance or gymnastic classes.
- Go to school.
- Do homework.
- Attend church.
- Play with neighbors.
- Watch TV.
- Play video games.

Wow! You must be very busy! We all fill each day with lots of activities.

The Bible says in Ephesians 5:15–16a, *"Be very careful, then, how you live—not as unwise but as wise, making the most of every opportunity."* So we know God cares about how we spend our time. He wants us to use our time wisely. God wants us to spend time doing things that are good and make Him happy—like learning about Him and sharing His love with others.

Today, make a schedule of when you will spend time learning about God. And make plans to do something special for someone else as a way to show your love for Jesus.

Prayer
God, help us fill our time with things that are good and that make You happy and teach others about You.

Making It Stick
Have the children create a calendar page for the current month, using the sample calendar and calendar sheets that you give them. Direct each child to add the dates of the month in the right squares and to fill the calendar with his or her weekly schedule, including time for

getting ready for school, attending school, doing homework, playing with friends, participating in extracurricular activities, attending church activities, watching TV, playing sports or video games, and whatever else they do.

Talk together about how the children use their time. Encourage them spend some time during the week to learn about God, to pray, and to do mission action projects.

Encourage children to create their own calendar at the beginning of every month.

Making It Personal
Memorize Ephesians 5:15–16*a*.

Set aside a few minutes each day this week to read your Bible and pray to God. Also spend some time doing something that reaches out to other people, such as a mission project, that shows the love of God to others.

Making It Home
Make a combined family calendar based on individual family member calendars that each of you has filled out. Evaluate the combined family calendar. Discuss ways you can use the hours in the day more wisely to make more time for learning about God and serving Him. Schedule family time weekly for a family chat or devotional. Consider incorporating a mission action project into the monthly schedule.

27

My Talents

Missional Message: God wants me to use my talents and gifts to honor Him.

Missional Challenge:
"Each one should use whatever gift he has received to serve others, faithfully administering God's grace in its various forms."
—1 Peter 4:10

What Is Needed: Bible, cooking utensils for illustration, paper, and pencils

Making It Real
(*Show children a few cooking utensils and describe the use for each of them.*)
These are a few of the things I use to cook with in the kitchen. Some of you may have parents or grandparents who are great cooks. (*Enlist a child or two to talk a little about someone in his or her family*

who is a great cook—what the person makes, what the child's favorite dish is, and so on. When the child finishes, ask the following question:) How does it make you feel when _____ (*name of the great cook*) cooks especially yummy food?

Yes, it makes you feel happy. God has given each of us special things that we can do. We call these things *talents* or *gifts*. Talents are abilities we have to do certain things well. Gifts are things that God gives to us to serve others. God wants us to use both our talents and our gifts to honor Him.

For example, some people are great cooks. These people can use their cooking talents in many ways. They can host parties for people to show God's love, cook for people who do not have food, or teach moms how to cook nutritious meals for their children. As you can see, there are many ways people can use cooking to serve others and show them the love of Jesus.

Another example would be using the gift of encouragement to honor God. When you encourage someone, you make that person feel special and loved. Someone with the gift of encouragement might send people cards for no reason but to say that they care, make a phone call to someone who was not at church to see how that person is doing. These encouragers are the people who are first to show care and concern to others in times of need.

Not everyone has the gift of encouragement or the talent to cook great meals. God made each of us differently. He wants us to use our gifts and talents to honor Him and serve others.

Prayer
God, thank You for giving each of us gifts and talents.

Making It Stick
Make a list of three things you do well. Then next to the list, write about or draw a picture of how you can use these talents or gifts to serve others.

Making It Personal
Memorize 1 Peter 4:10.

Put into practice this week one of the talents or gifts you put on your list to serve someone else.

Making It Home

Have each family member write down three things he or she does well. Share the lists with one another. Encourage family members to serve others by implementing at least one of the gifts. Plan a family mission action project on which family members all work together sharing individual gifts and/or talents to minister to others.

My Money

Missional Message: God wants me to use my money wisely.

Missional Challenge:
"Keep your lives free from the love of money and be content with what you have, because God has said, 'Never will I leave you; never will I forsake you.'"
—Hebrews 13:5

What Is Needed: Box filled with lots of dollar bills or play money and covered with a lid.

Making It Real
(*Show the children the box that is full of money but has a lid hiding the contents.*)

I have something special in this box. (*Open the box.*)
Wow, everyone got really excited about seeing all that money!
Do you think God gives us money? The Bible says that all things come from God (Ecclesiastes 11:5; James 1:17; Revelation 4:11).

Raise your hand if you think money is good. Raise your hand if you think money is bad. Money is both good and bad. Money can be very useful, but the Bible says the love of money is a root of all kinds of evil (1 Timothy 6:10).

(Read Hebrews 13:5.) God encourages us not to love money and to be content with what we have. We need to be good caretakers––the Bible calls someone who takes good care of something a *steward*. We need to take good care of what God gives us, and that includes money.

God wants us to use money wisely on the things that help us and other people to know Jesus better. God wants us to use our money to support the work of the church and its mission.

Prayer
God, may we be good caretakers of the money You give us. And help us to be content with what we have.

Making It Stick
Say the following statements to the children, and ask them to respond as to whether they think these are ways God would want us to spend our money. You could take a show of hands or vote if desired.
- Give money to help someone in need.
- Buy an expensive pair of jeans.
- Buy a music player.
- Buy brand-name shoes.
- Buy a friend a present.
- Give money to the church.
- Buy a dog.
- Buy a new computer game.
- Save money.
- Buy toys.

Lead a discussion on being content with what we have.

Making It Personal
Memorize Hebrews 13:5.

This month, save the money that you would have spent on snacks, toys, or clothes, and give it to someone in need.

Making It Home

As a family, discuss what Hebrews 13:5 means to family finances. Make a list of all the items on which the family spends money. Discuss ways that the family can cut back on spending in order to be better stewards of God's blessings. After tithing, commit to saving money. Give more to people in need and to Christian ministry.

My Tithe

Missional Message: God expects me to tithe.

Missional Challenge:
"'Bring the whole tithe into the storehouse, that there may be food in my house. Test me in this,' says the LORD Almighty, 'and see if I will not throw open the floodgates of heaven and pour out so much blessing that you will not have room enough for it.'"
—Malachi 3:10

What Is Needed: Bible, 20 dimes, offering plate, and pretend money

Making It Real

How many of you have heard the word *tithe*? *(Write it on a dry wipe board or blackboard if you have one.)* This word is in the Bible. *(Read Malachi 3:10.)* A *tithe* equals ten percent of what we have, including our time and money. The *storehouse* means "God's house." So God is saying that He wants us to bring a tithe, ten percent, to Him. God wants us to give ten percent to build His house, or what we would call "the church." But remember, the church is the people, not the building.

So let me show you what a tithe is by using these ten dimes. *(Count out ten dimes.)*

I have ten dimes. Ten percent of one dollar is ten cents or one dime. That means for a tithe, I would actually take a dime from every dollar that I get and give it to the church. *(Place one dime in the offering plate and the remaining change in your pocket. Get out the additional 10 dimes.)* Look, I have another ten more dimes. *(Place another dime in the offering plate and put the remaining change in your pocket.)* Twenty cents of my two dollars will go toward supporting the work of the church.

God wants us to give money to Him first and then keep the rest to use in ways that are honoring to God.

Prayer
God, thank You for all that You give me. Help me to remember to give back to You my tithe.

Making It Stick
Tell the children how your church uses the tithes that come in from every family.

Pass out to each child $10 worth of pretend money in either $1 bills or lesser change. Have each child write down a plan for how they should spend the $10. Encourage the children to separate out the tithe first and to also set aside some money to support missions. Discuss how they can support God's work with their allowances, money-gifts they receive, or earnings.

Making It Personal
Memorize Malachi 3:10.

Starting this month (if you have not started already), for every dollar that you are given or earn, give ten cents to the church.

Making It Home
As a family, discuss tithing. Set up a family budget that encourages members to tithe and to give to missions. Celebrate with stories of how God has blessed your family through tithing.

My Speech

Missional Message: God cares about what I say.

Missional Challenge:
"May the words of my mouth and the meditation of my heart be pleasing in your sight, O LORD, my Rock and my Redeemer."
—Psalm 19:14

What Is Needed: Bible and a doll that "talks"

Making It Real
I brought a doll to share with you all. This is a special doll because it talks. (*Tell a little about what the doll says. Then show the children how the doll works.*)

This doll says the same few things over and over again. God created us to be able to say lots of different words and phases. Through our words, we tell others how we feel and what we think. We communicate to others what is in our minds.

Do you think God cares what we say? Almost 100 verses in

the Bible use the word *tongue*. I will read a few of them. (*Read the following verses from the Bible.*)
- 1 Peter 3:10
- Psalm 35:28
- Proverbs 12:18

According to these verses, our words, spoken with our tongues, can be evil, dishonest, or out of control, but what we say can also bring healing to others and praise to God. These verses show that you can use your words two ways—for good or for bad.

What happens when someone says something mean or full of hate to us? It makes us sad or mad. What happens when someone says something positive or full of love to us? It makes us happy or cheers us up.

Psalm 19:14 says, *"May the words of my mouth and the meditation of my heart be pleasing in your sight, O Lord, my Rock and my Redeemer."* God wants our words and thoughts to be pleasing to Him. The words you say come from the thoughts you think. If you think good thoughts, then good words will come from your mouth. On the other hand, if you think bad thoughts, bad words will come from your mouth.

What you say and think is important to God. Through our words, people get a good idea of what we are thinking. God wants people to hear good words coming from our mouths—words that let other people know that we love them and care for them.

Prayer
God, thank You for the ability to speak. May what we say please You.

Making It Stick
Let the children decide whether the following statements are words they should be speaking:
- I do not like to be around you.
- Your clothes look funny.
- I like playing with you.
- You do not know what you are talking about.

- You are nice.
- That is stupid.
- You are mean.
- You are a tattletale.

Discuss how children can respond when they hear other children saying words like these.

Making It Personal
Memorize Psalm 19:14.

Have you said something mean to someone in the past month? Go and ask that person to forgive you. Each time, before you speak, ask yourself this question: *Are these words pleasing to God?*

Making It Home
Look up other Scriptures in the Bible about speech.

Make family rules that specify how you communicate to one another in the home, ranging from words of encouragement to fighting fair. Hold one another accountable to help ensure your speech is pleasing to God.

31
My Testimony

Missional Message: God wants me to share my testimony with others.

Missional Challenge:
"I am not ashamed of the gospel, because it is the power of God for the salvation of everyone who believes: first for the Jew, then for the Gentile."
—Romans 1:16

What Is Needed: Bible, paper, markers, and fasteners for booklets

Making It Real

I am going to make some facial expressions. I want you to guess what I am feeling. (*Express happiness. Express sadness. Express embarrassment.*)

Have you ever felt embarrassed or ashamed? Sure, we have all felt that way at some time in life. For example, how many of you have said or done something silly and then wished you could pretend it had never happened or that no one had heard you? Did you feel like you wanted to run and hide? I will share what happened to me one time: I fell down, and I was so upset! I hoped no one had seen me! I wanted to run and hide. I felt so embarrassed!

Here is what the Bible says: (*Read Romans 1:16*) God does not want us to be ashamed of or embarrassed by Him. He does not want us to hide our love for and belief in Him from other people. In fact, God wants us to tell others about Jesus boldly. We can tell about Jesus's life, death, and coming back to life. And we can tell about what Jesus means to each of us. This Bible verse tells us that it is important that we tell others so that they may believe in Jesus and be saved by Him. (*Read also Matthew 28:19–20, Mark 5:19, John 20:31, and Romans 10:14 if time allows.*)

This week, tell your parents all that you know about Jesus and what He means to you. Then tell a friend.

Prayer
God, thank You for all that You have done. Help us to be bold as we tell others about You.

Making It Stick
Ask children why they think that some people might be embarrassed or ashamed to share about Jesus. Discuss ways that children can share Jesus with others.

Have the children write or draw a picture in a booklet with a page to represent each of the following statements:
- Jesus loves me.
- Jesus died for me.
- Jesus wants me to obey the Bible.
- Jesus cares about everyone.

Have children share what Jesus has done for them.

Making It Personal
Memorize Romans 1:16.

Share the booklet you made with some friends.

Making It Home
Tell your children what Jesus means to you. Help them to verbalize what Jesus means to them. Take time this month to read through the Book of Luke.

32

My Friends

Missional Message: God cares about my friendships.

Missional Challenge:
"As iron sharpens iron, so one man sharpens another."
—Proverbs 27:17

What Is Needed: Bible, optional iron tool such as a carpenter's file if you have one available

Making It Real

I am going to ask you a yes or no question. I would like you to respond by nodding your head for yes or shaking it for no. Does God care about your friendships?

Yes, God does care about your friendships. The Bible says in Proverbs 12:26 that we should choose our friends carefully, because our friends can lead us to do the wrong things. *(Read the verse.)* Also, our verse for today, Proverbs 27:17, uses a picture of something you might do in a workshop, to explain to us that our friends make us stronger. Have any of you ever worked in a workshop with a grownup? Sometimes you might use an iron sharpener to make an iron tool work better. (*Show the file.*) Sharpening iron against iron is a good way to put both the tool (file) and its sharpener to their best uses.

These two verses show us that the friendships we make influence what we believe and how we act. A friend who does bad things can lead us to do bad things. At the same time, a friend who does good things can help us to be a better person and even be a better follower of Jesus.

I am going to make a few statements about being a friend. If the statement describes a way of being a good friend, nod yes. If the statement pictures being a not-so-good friend, shake your head for no.
- Friends are mean.
- Friends are kind.
- Friends say mean things about you.
- Friends tear up your toys on purpose.
- Friends help you.

Not only do we need to have good friends but we need friends that help us be better followers of Jesus.

Prayer
God, help us make friends with those who help us be better people. And help us to be a good friend to our friends.

Making It Stick
Read to the children the following Scripture passages: 1 Corinthians 4:17 and 1 Samuel 18:1–4.

Help children identify what the traits of true friendship are through the words of Paul about Timothy and through the story of David and Jonathan. For example, Paul's comments about Timothy and the story of the friendship between David and Jonathan demonstrate respect, admiration, and shared belief in God and in Jesus.

Have children state what they need to look for in a friend.

Making It Personal
Memorize Proverbs 27:17.

Make a list of your top five friends. Ask yourself if these people help you to be a better follower of Jesus Christ. If not, how can you change the situation so that you are helping one another serve God?

Making It Home
Discuss with your children why you have the friends you have. Tell how your friends help you follow Christ. To help children talk about their friends, have them draw a picture of their friends and them hanging out together. Have them explain the picture and share characteristics about their friends.

Go to People

Missional Message: God wants Christians to tell all people about Jesus.

Missional Challenge:
"Therefore go and make disciples of all nations, baptizing them in the name of the Father and of the Son and of the Holy Spirit."
—Matthew 28:19

What Is Needed: Bible map of the world or United States, backpack, pictures of people of different cultures, ball, and a foreign language book, a cookbook with recipes from other countries, and/or a book about people of different cultures, optional Bible printed in a language other than English.

Making It Real

What nation do you live in? One word for "nation" is *country*. You live in the nation, or country, of the *United States*. (*Show children their country on the map.*)

Jesus tells us in the Bible that He wants us to go to all nations to tell people about Jesus. (*Read Matthew 28:19.*) The word *nations* can also mean "people groups." By that we mean people who share beliefs about God with people from homes and families that are similar to theirs. Their beliefs are often very different from our beliefs, and we want them to know about Jesus.

You may be thinking, *When I grow up, I can go to other countries and tell people about Jesus. But now, I am just a child. How can I tell the world about Jesus?*

Sometimes "going to nations" does not just mean going to different countries. It can also mean going to a people group in our own country. People groups from all over the world have come to *United States* (*name of children's country*). We can go out into our cities and be among several nations or people groups in one day.

I have a backpack with a few things in it that can help you understand how *you* can go to all people groups. (*Display backpack.*)

- We can pray. (*Show a picture or two of someone of a different culture.*) When we see pictures of people around the world we can pray for them.
- We can learn about people groups. (*Show the cookbook, foreign language book, or book about people of other cultures.*
- We can befriend others. (*Show a ball.*) There are children from different people groups in our neighborhood and school. They need friends to help them adjust to living in a new place. You can be their friend.
- We can provide Bibles for others to learn about God. (*Show a Bible—if you have one in another language available, show it, too.*) We can share God's love by giving others Bibles or helping support ministries that distribute Bibles.

Can you think of a person you know who is of a different people group? Pray for that person. Learn about the person's way of life. Look for ways to be a friend to that person. Share a Bible with that person. Teach that person about Jesus. Then when that person returns to their relatives in another country, they can tell them about Jesus.

Prayer
God, help us to be a friend to children from other people groups.

Making It Stick
Make a list of all the people the children know who are from different people groups. Then have the children draw pictures representing ways they can be friends to the persons listed. Also have them brainstorm ways they can share the love of Jesus so those persons would learn about Jesus.

Making It Personal
Memorize Matthew 28:19.

Write or illustrate what you would teach about Jesus to your friends from other people groups. Scripture verses such as John 3:16; John 10:10; and Romans 10:8–10 can help children, especially older children, know what to say.

Making It Home
Help your children to develop positive points of view about people from different cultural backgrounds. If you know a family from another people group, invite that family into your home to share their culture and even religious beliefs with you and your family. Use this opportunity to discuss with your children your faith and why you believe as you do. Teaching your children the difference between what the Bible says and what other belief systems teach will prepare them to discern biblical truth later in life. Visit www.peoplegroups.info to learn about people groups in your community.

Go to the World

34

Missional Message: God gives us the Holy Spirit and the direction to go and tell.

Missional Challenge:
"But you will receive power when the Holy Spirit comes on you; and you will be my witnesses in Jerusalem, and in all Judea and Samaria, and to the ends of the earth."
—Acts 1:8

What Is Needed: Bible and dry wipe board or poster with three concentric circles drawn on it, blank paper with optional patterns or plastic bowls in graduated sizes for them to trace onto the paper

Making It Real
(Show the children the three concentric circles, similar to a target, which you have drawn on a piece of poster board or on a dry wipe board.)

I am going to use these circles to illustrate the last thing that Jesus told His disciples before He went to heaven. In the Bible verse Acts 1:8, Jesus told His disciples that they will receive power from the Holy Spirit to go and witness to the world what He has done.

Jesus gave His followers instructions on how to go and tell others. He began with the city of Jerusalem. Let's pretend this middle circle is Jerusalem. You see, Jerusalem is where they were and that is where Jesus and His disciples taught the people of the Jewish faith, who were from the same neighborhoods as they. There are also many people around here in our own neighborhoods who do not know Jesus. God wants us to go and tell those people about Jesus.

Then the next place He talked about was Judea. This is the area of country around Jerusalem. That area could be the next circle. Many Jewish people also lived in Judea. These people lived and acted very much like the disciples, but they had not yet heard about Jesus. Jesus wanted the disciples to go to these people and tell them about Him.

Then the next place Jesus named was Samaria. The next circle, the outside circle, could represent Samaria. In that country were people who did not think or act like the disciples. Jesus told His disciples to go to people who were different from them and tell them about Him.

Then Jesus also said, "to the ends of the earth." In other words, He was saying, "I do not want you just to stop with the people who are different from you; I want you to go to all the world." The area outside all the circles represents the whole world. Jesus wanted and still wants everyone in the world to hear about Him.

The Book of Acts in the New Testament is a record of the adventures the disciples had as they did what Jesus said to do. They waited and God sent the Holy Spirit to help them. Then they began to move outward, to tell others about Jesus.

God wants us to continue to do what the disciples did today. He wants us to move outside these circles and tell people about Jesus. Or if we ourselves cannot go, we can help support Christian teachers and preachers in other countries or missionaries that we send to tell other people about Jesus.

Prayer

God, thank You for giving us the Holy Spirit and instructions on how to tell others about Jesus.

Making It Stick

Show the children how to draw concentric circles. Help them to fill in the blank areas with the people who represent each circle. To make this easier to understand, you can suggest that the inner circle (Jerusalem) represents your neighborhood, such as your school, your street or your children's group, the middle circle (Judea) is your state or region, and the larger circle (Samaria) could be your country or the rest of the world.

Making It Personal

Memorize Acts 1:8.

Review your paper with the circles drawn on it. Create ways that you can tell each group about Jesus. Record your thoughts in the circles on your paper.

Making It Home

As a family, discuss how you can minister to people in the different places listed in Acts 1:8. Plan family mission action projects for each area this year.

III
Missions

Missions Education

35

Missional Message: God wants us to learn about missions.

Missional Challenge:
"Do you not say, 'Four months more and then the harvest'? I tell you, open your eyes and look at the fields! They are ripe for harvest."
—John 4:35

What Is Needed: Bible, fruit or vegetable that farmers grow in your region, signs for illustrations, paper for each child, and pencils

Making It Real
How many of you have been taught to read? How many of you are just learning to read? Learning to read is a very important thing, because reading is necessary to be able to do everything from buying groceries to shopping for clothes to surfing the Internet. It is the one tool that you use every day of your life.

Just like learning to read is important, so is learning about doing missions. We learn about missions by both reading and doing.

Let's think of the ways we learn about missions and the ways that we do missions. (*Hold up signs one at a time that are imprinted with* LEARNING, SEEING, DOING, SUPPORTING, *and* PRAYING, *and talk about each point in turn.*)

- **Learning**—We learn what the Bible says about God and His mission to the world.
- **Seeing**–We witness how God is working around the world through the stories and actions of missionaries and national Christians.
- **Doing**—We do mission projects through our actions and words in our own community and city.
- **Supporting**—We give our time, personal belongings, or money to help people know about Jesus.
- **Praying**—We pray for people who do not know Jesus and we pray for people who do missions.

(*Show the vegetable or fruit to the children.*) Jesus compares going and telling people about Him to bringing in food during the harvest season. In John 4:35, Jesus says, *"Do you not say, 'Four months more and then the harvest'? I tell you, open your eyes and look at the fields! They are ripe for harvest."* This means that people are ready to know about Jesus, but someone needs to go tell them about Him.

When we see the needs, we should respond by praying, supporting, and doing something about them.

Prayer
God, thank You for giving us resources to learn about missions. Help us to grow in our understanding of You and Your mission for Christ followers.

Making It Stick
Give each child a sheet of paper with the phrases below printed on it. Privately assign one of the actions to each child to act out, and then

let the other children guess which of the areas the child is portraying. Have the children write beside each statement how they would study and learn more about these areas. A great Web site for children's missions education is www.childrensmissions.com.

- Learning the Bible
- Learning about missions
- Praying for missions
- Doing missions (mission action and witnessing)
- Giving to missions

Making It Personal
Memorize John 4:35.

Make a missions scrapbook of all the things you know about missions. Complete information about the missionaries you have met or look up information about them on the Internet and attach what you find into your scrapbook, or write a paragraph about them. Include pictures of you and others doing missions. Display pictures of people and places that need to have missionaries. Keep a daily record of the times you pray for people doing missions and a record of how you see God working in your church.

Making It Home
As a family, create a missions education lesson for your home from the information you find on www.childrensmissions.com, www.joshuaproject.com, and other missions sites.

Missiology

Missional Message: God wants Christians to do missions.

Missional Challenge:
"For Christ's love compels us, because we are convinced that one died for all, and therefore all died."
—2 Corinthians 5:14

What Is Needed: Bible and children's toys

Making It Real

(*Show the children some toys.*) I almost tripped on these toys at home [or church] this morning. Someone did not pick up his [or her] toys.

I have a question for you. After I ask you the question, I am going to give you two possible answers. I want you to decide which is the correct answer for you.

Question: Why do you do pick up your toys when you are finished playing? Raise your hand if you agree with either of these two answers:

- I clean up my toys because my mom or dad asked me to do so.
- I clean up my toys because I want to do so.

Did some of you raise your hand both times? A few of you may clean up your toys for both reasons.

It is amazing, but these two reasons are similar to the reasons we do missions: we do them because God tells us to do missions and because we want to do missions.

In the Bible, one of the last things Jesus did before going to heaven was to tell His disciples to go and make disciples of all nations (Matthew 28:19–20). Jesus wanted His disciples to tell others about Him so that others would have the opportunity to know and follow Him.

Jesus's disciples obeyed what Jesus had told them to do. They began traveling to different places to tell others about Jesus. They started churches in homes and temples so that new followers of Jesus would have a place to come to learn and worship God.

The Apostle Paul also told many people about Jesus. Some people did mean things to try to stop Paul, but he kept right on going. *(Read 2 Corinthians 5:14.)* Paul is saying that Jesus's love for him compels him—the word *compels* means something like "makes him want to go"—to tell others. No matter how hard it was, Paul wanted to tell others about Jesus.

Like Paul, we should do missions because God tells us to and because we feel compelled by the love that God has shown us. We want to share that love with others.

Prayer
God, thank You for Your love for us. Help us to have the same excitement as Paul did, as we share Jesus's love with others.

Making It Stick
Invite a missionary and a minister to come share why they are Christ followers and what they do to spread the love of Jesus.

Making It Personal
Memorize 2 Corinthians 5:14.

Make a list of your three favorite activities. Pray to God asking Him to increase your desire to do missions so it will move into or up to the top of that list.

Making It Home
As a family, research the words *mission, missions,* and *missional* on the Internet or in the library or local bookstore. Make a file with the information the family collects. Discuss the wide range of activities that missions organizations and churches are doing. Web sites of interest include www.worldmap.org and www.billygrahamcenter.com.

Missionaries

37

Missional Message: God uses missionaries to tell about Jesus.

Missional Challenge:
"Day after day, in the temple courts and from house to house, they never stopped teaching and proclaiming the good news that Jesus is the Christ."
—Acts 5:42

What Is Needed: Bible and world globe, pictures of missionaries in various vocations if available, blackboard, dry wipe board or poster board

Making It Real
(*Show the children a globe.*) Some people go to different places all over the world to tell others about Jesus. These people are called *missionaries*. A missionary is a person who feels that God has asked him or her to go tell others about Jesus. There are missionaries all over the world. Missionaries come from lots of different countries.

(*Demonstrate the meaning of these next two sentences by pointing to places on the globe.*) Some missionaries may stay in their own area—maybe in our own city or neighborhood—to share Jesus's love with people. Other missionaries may move to another country and learn a new language to minister to different people groups.

Missionaries use their skills, talents, and education to tell others about Jesus. (*Show pictures if you have them.*) There are many different jobs that missionaries can do. For example, a missionary could be a filmmaker, a businessperson, a nurse, a pastor, a social worker, a teacher, a coach, or a surfer. Yes, I said a surfer. We know of at least one missionary who uses his surfing skills as a way to make friends with people on the beach and share about Jesus with his new friends.

The Book of Acts in the Bible tells us about the first times that missionaries spread out to share the good news of Jesus with people who did not know about Him. Acts 5:42 gives us a look into their lives. (*Read the Scripture.*) Missionaries continually spend their skills, talents, and time to minister to people so that they will know Jesus.

God may want one of you to be a missionary one day. For now, we can support missionaries by praying for them and encouraging them with letters.

Prayer
God, thank You for missionaries. Help us to hear Your call to serve You.

Making It Stick
Have children brainstorm about the different types of jobs missionaries might have. Then have them think about ways that missionaries could tell about Jesus as they do each of the jobs the children listed. Make a list on a blackboard, dry wipe board, or poster board and hang it on the wall.

Making It Personal
Memorize Acts 5:42.

You may not be an official missionary, but you can live like a missionary each day. Ask God to help you be like a missionary and look for ways to share Jesus daily by using your gifts and talents to help others.

Send a letter of encouragement to a missionary.

Making It Home

Invite a missionary or someone who has been on a mission trip to dinner. Have that person share about what he or she is doing to tell others about Jesus. Encourage the children to talk with the person after dinner.

Church Planting

Missional Message: God wants us to go and start new churches.

Missional Challenge:
"How, then, can they call on the one they have not believed in? And how can they believe in the one of whom they have not heard? And how can they hear without someone preaching to them?"
—Romans 10:14

What Is Needed: Bible, pictures of churches that meet in unusual or surprising places, review of the hand illustrations for "This Is the Church," poster board, paper, and pencils

Making It Real
(*Do the hand signs to this rhyme.*)

This is the church,
This the steeple,
Look inside and here are the people.

This is a very old rhyme that, at the end, tells what is important about the church—the people. The church is the people, not the building. The building is a place where the people meet to learn, fellowship, and worship God. But the church does not need a building to be a church.

Today there are pastors and missionaries in our community and all around the world who are starting churches by bringing groups of people together to learn about Jesus. The groups begin to grow into churches when the people attending these Bible studies become followers of Jesus and begin worshipping God together.

These churches are even being started in some countries where it is against the law to have Christian meetings, in towns where people do not feel safe going into a church building that looks like ours, and in cities where few Christians live.

Our verse for today, Romans 10:14, says, *"How, then, can they call on the one they have not believed in? And how can they believe in the one of whom they have not heard? And how can they hear without someone preaching to them?"*

Remember the people who represent the church? (*Wiggle your fingers in the air with your hands separated from one another.*) One group is a group who knows about Jesus, and the other group does not. Jesus wants the group who knows about Him to go to the people over here and share about Jesus. This is how churches get started. (*Pull your fingers together to once again represent the church.*)

Churches start when people who know Jesus share the good news about Jesus with other people who need to know Him. They teach others about Jesus so that those people also can take the message of Jesus to even more people. And that's how new churches get started and also how churches grow.

Prayer
God, we pray that the followers of Christ will go to others to teach them about Jesus and start new churches.

Making It Stick
Pose these questions to children: If you could create your own church,

what would it look like? Would you sing songs? How would you learn? Some church meeting places look very different from ours, but the people want to learn about Jesus just like we do. *(If you have pictures of church meeting places that don't fit the stereotype, such as a house, a storefront, a school building, or the outdoors, show them to the children.)*

Write the children's descriptions on a poster board. Then have children create a picture of the church based on the descriptions.

Making It Personal
Memorize Romans 10:14.

Evaluate how many people in your neighborhood go to church. Why do people go to church? Have you asked a neighbor to go to your church? Why or why not?

Making It Home
Discuss as a family how you can use your home as a place to teach others about Jesus and bring others into the church family. Plan and host a neighborhood party at your home. Invite your neighbors to your church or a home Bible study. Consider hosting a Backyard Bible Club in the summer.

Evangelism

Missional Message: Christ followers share the good news.

Missional Challenge:
"But he said, 'I must preach the good news of the kingdom of God to the other towns also, because that is why I was sent.'"
—Luke 4:43

What Is Needed: Bible, poster or posters with magazine cut-outs that illustrate the types of evangelism, information with pictures if possible about how your church does evangelism, paper for children to make a one-page newsletter, and markers

Making It Real
(*Sing the chorus of the song "Tell the Good News" or "Go Tell It on the Mountain."*)

What good news is the song referring to? Do you remember the angels who sang to the shepherds out in the field when the baby Jesus was born? They sang about good news. What good news were they singing about? Yes, the good news is about Jesus. Luke 4:43 tells us that Jesus came to earth to preach the good news of God's kingdom. He wants us to tell the good news too. Another word for telling the good news is *evangelism*.

Let's discuss three examples of evangelism. *(Show the poster.)*

- *Friendship Evangelism:* Christ followers are sharing Jesus with their friends. They are making an effort to meet new friends so they can teach them about Jesus. For instance, when missionaries move to a new place, they spend time getting to know people that are around them. They build friendships with these people. Through the friendships, they are able to help people and share what they believe about Jesus.
- *Door-to-Door Evangelism:* Christ followers are going door-to-door in some neighborhoods, telling the people about Jesus and inviting them to church. For instance, some churches go to houses in their community to get to know people and to invite them to church. Sometimes there is an opportunity to tell them about Jesus at the first meeting.
- *Event Evangelism:* Church groups are sponsoring events in communities for children and/or adults who might not attend church and sharing about Jesus at these events. For instance, churches are sponsoring sports leagues and inviting the community to participate. At every opportunity, children and parents are being taught about Jesus.

These are just a few ways that individuals and groups are doing evangelism. Our church is doing evangelism by . . . *(Share how your church is telling people about Jesus.)*

Prayer
God, thank You for the good news of Jesus. Show us how we can tell our community about Your good news.

Making It Stick
Discuss ways children in your group can tell others about Jesus. Have each child make a colorful one-page newsletter that tells about Jesus through words or pictures. Encourage the children to give their newsletter to another child.

Making It Personal
Memorize Luke 4:43.
   Share the newsletter you made with a friend outside of church.

Making It Home
Talk with family members about what the good news means. Encourage one another to tell someone about Jesus this week. Then get together and discuss as a family the experiences you each had.

Partnership Missions 40

Missional Message: God wants us to partner with others to share Jesus.

Missional Challenge:
"Your love has given me great joy and encouragement, because you, brother, have refreshed the hearts of the saints."
—Philemon 7

What Is Needed: Bible and jar with lid, information about your church's mission partnerships, world globe or map if available, card stock paper and markers, pencils, and/or crayons, optional stickers

Making It Real
(*Pretend to not be able to open a lid on a jar.*) I need a partner. Can someone help me open this jar? (*Ask a child to hold the bottom while you unscrew the lid.*)

That was much easier when I had someone else helping me.

Churches are realizing that it is easier to tell people about Jesus when they work with other churches.

Small churches and big churches alike are partnering with other churches around the world to support the work of God. *(If your church has a mission partnership, share a couple of sentences about the partnership and how lives are being changed.)*

Here is an example of how churches can be partners with each other: Southside Baptist Church in Alabama partnered with Lanzarote Baptist Church in the Canary Islands of Spain. *(If you have a map or globe, point out where the Canary Islands are.)* Throughout the partnership, small groups from the United States would take short-term trips to the Canary Islands to encourage people and help in several ways. People from the church in Alabama helped to train new church leaders and they held special men's and women's prayer meetings. They also helped with children's programs and sports programs. And they got together with the Canary Islands church members to do prayerwalking and door-to-door evangelism. The pastor from the church in the Canary Islands came all the way to Alabama to do a revival. Over the five years of the partnership, the church in the Canary Islands grew from about 15 people to more than 200, with many different small groups meeting all over the island. The church had members from Spain, Brazil, Germany, England, and many other countries. The church in Alabama grew in its understanding of and passion for missions. Both churches benefited from the partnership.*

Churches also often partner with a missions organization to pray for people groups or missionaries in certain places. Some churches have adopted places that do not have missionaries or Christian people in the community. These churches are praying for those communities and sending short-term mission teams to the areas, and, in some cases, the churches also send and support church members to be in the countries for longer periods as missionaries to spread the message of Jesus.

The Bible encourages these partnerships. In the Book of Philemon, the Apostle Paul says, *"Your love has given me great joy and encouragement, because you, brother, have refreshed the hearts of the saints."* When Paul uses the word *saints*, he means "followers of Jesus." This is an example from the Bible of different groups of believers encouraging and supporting one another. We can begin encouraging other churches through prayer. We can also ask God to provide opportunities for our church to partner with other churches in missions.

Prayer
God, thank You that groups of believers can encourage and support one another in missions.

Making It Stick
Discuss the importance of individuals and churches working together to encourage and support one another. Teach the children about your church's mission partnerships. Allow time for the children to make cheerful and colorful cards to send to your church's partner churches and collect them for sending. Pray for the partnerships.

Making It Personal
Memorize Philemon 7.

Uplift the leaders in your church with a note of encouragement to each of them. Copy this verse and include it in your notes.

Making It Home
Create a partnership of encouragement and support with another family. Meet together and plan a missions action project. Do the missions action project this month.

*Story provided from author's personal experience while serving at Southside Baptist Church, Southside, Alabama. (Joe and Chari, you are the best!)

41 Technology

Missional Message: God wants us to use our resources to reach others for Christ.

Missional Challenge:
"We write this to make our joy complete."
—1 John 1:4

What Is Needed: Bible, laptop computer or hand-held computer device, and/or camera phone

Making It Real

In Bible days, followers of Christ used letter-writing to tell others about Jesus. The Apostle Paul continually communicated to the churches through letters. Communicating about Jesus to others gave Paul joy. In 1 John 1, we see that the Apostle John also shared about Jesus through letters. In verse 4, he stated, *"We write this to make our joy complete."*

(*Show the children a laptop computer or hand-held device.*) Today, we communicate much faster. To get a message to another church in the times of Paul took many days, weeks, and even months, but today I can communicate anywhere in the world within seconds. I can email as many people as my computer will allow within seconds at one click of a button. I can take a picture of this group and send it to a missionary on the other side of the world with a message saying we are praying for that missionary. (*If your hand-held takes pictures, take a snapshot of the children that you can email to a missionary.*) And the missionary can respond and thank us for praying for him or her. I can download a movie or television show and watch it from my computer in minutes. The world of technological communication is at our fingertips.

The world is connected by technology. How do we use this technology to tell people about Jesus? What ways can you think of? (*Allow time for responses—children are savvy about ways you may not even think of!*) Here are few more things we can do:

- Text message your friends Scripture verses and prayers.
- Make a video with your family and upload it to YouTube or have a neighborhood viewing party.
- Create a family Web site or blog to share your faith.
- Purchase your favorite Christian songs from the Internet and burn CDs for your friends. (Make sure that you are following laws and regulations about copying music if you do this.)
- Have a movie-screening party. After viewing the movie, discuss it and end the night with a Bible devotional.
- Have a Bible study group that meets online during the week.

You'll probably think of even more new and amazing ways to tell others about Jesus through technology.

Prayer
God, thank You for giving us technology. Help us to use it to tell others about You.

Making It Stick

Review the different technologies listed, and have children brainstorm ways they can put technology to use in sharing their faith with these tools:

- Radio
- TV
- Films and movies
- Music
- Live theater programs
- Computers
- Video games
- Web sites

Making It Personal

Memorize 1 John 1:4.

Paul and John, disciples of Jesus, wrote letters. What do you like to do? How can you use the technology you have available to share Jesus?

Making It Home

As a family, visit University of the Nations at Kona, www.uofnkona.edu, or another Web site that describes the various ways a college or university prepares Christians through technology to share the good news of Jesus Christ. On the University of the Nations at Kona site click on "Colleges/Faculties and Centers" and then on "Communication" to read about all the programs the school has. Using technology, do a family project to share about Jesus.

Children

Missional Message: God works through children.

Missional Challenge:
"Jesus said, 'Let the little children come to me, and do not hinder them, for the kingdom of heaven belongs to such as these.'"
—Matthew 19:14

What Is Needed: Bible, empty shoe box, shoe box ready for Operation Christmas Child, items collected for children to fill boxes, wrapping paper, scotch tape, scissors, and a shoe box for each child, paper for poems or drawings

Making It Real
(*Show children an empty shoe box.*) Do you think this shoe box can change a child's life?
 (*Then pull out a shoe box that has been packed with gifts for a child and wrapped.*) Do you think this shoe box can change a child's life?

There are children all over the world who are very poor. They do not get enough to eat, much less Christmas presents. However, each of us can make a difference in a child's life by doing something as simple and easy as preparing a box of gifts for a child. Since 1993, Operation Christmas Child has been sending boxes that individuals and church groups have prepared for children throughout the world.

A girl named Shamila from Pakistan was grateful that she received a toothbrush in her box. She had never used a toothbrush. She said it was beautiful.

These gifts provide children with necessary items, school supplies, and toys that their families could never afford to buy their children.

Each of the Operation Christmas Child gift boxes is distributed by a Christian group in various countries. The churches and groups invite the children to attend a party. Then at the party, all the children get a Christmas present and gospel storybook. Often the children are asked to come back and go through a series of lessons about the Bible. Many children who receive the gift boxes begin coming to the church and learning about Jesus.

Andrea, age 10, said, "The Operation Christmas Child gifts impacted me very much. I had the opportunity to find the way to Jesus, and with the Bible course, I learned that God gave His Son to die on the Cross for my sins."

Giving the Operation Christmas Child gifts helps the church or ministry to show Jesus's love to people. Jesus says in Matthew 19:14, _____. (*Read the verse.*) Jesus wants the children of the world to know Him.

Prayer
God, I pray that many children around the world will come to know You through the gifts that they receive in shoe boxes through Operation Christmas Child.

Making It Stick
Have children prepare Operation Christmas Child gift boxes. Encourage the children to include the church address so the recipient will have the opportunity to write them back. You may include

information about your group, such as pictures and letters from the children.

Making It Personal
Memorize Matthew 19:14.

How does the special emphasis that Jesus puts on children make you feel? Create a poem or picture that expresses your feelings. Put your poem in the gift box you prepared.

Making It Home
Talk to your children about the many basics they have—toothbrushes, combs, shoelaces, soap, tissues, and other items—that they think of as necessities. Many people around the world do not have even these basic items. As a family, discuss how you can help other children in your community and in the world. Consider helping a needy family purchase food and gifts for Christmas. For more information about Operation Christmas Child visit http://www.samaritanspurse.org/default.asp.

Animals

Missional Message: God can use goats!

Missional Challenge:
"If you spend yourselves in behalf of the hungry and satisfy the needs of the oppressed, then your light will rise in the darkness, and your night will become like the noonday."
—Isaiah 58:10

What Is Needed: Bible, pictures of farm animals, paper, and crayons, world globe or map if available

Making It Real

I brought some pictures to show you about missions. (*Show the children pictures of goats, cows, pigs, and chickens, or other farm animals.*)

Have you ever thought of farm animals as being a part of missions? Let me share two examples of how Christ followers are using goats to do God's missions.

There is a country called Croatia across the Atlantic Ocean from the United States. *(Point it out if you have a map or globe available.)* After years of war in Croatia, which has left many families without money for food, clothing, and places to live, people are looking for ways to support their families. One missionary is helping these people by providing animals for farming. Families use the goats for making milk and cheese to support their families. In 2006, children's groups (Girls in Action® and Children in Action℠) from the United States sent more than $268,000 to help these families. The missionary is helping the people create businesses to sell cheese. As the missionary is helping the people financially, he is also telling them about Jesus.

Another example is a school in Africa called the Ricks Institute in Liberia, a Christian school for girls and boys. The average person in Liberia lives on about 50 cents a day, well below the world poverty line of $1 a day. The school provides free education for elementary-age children and three meals a week. The school relies on donations to pay the teachers and for the children's food. Recently, the school started an agricultural program. This is where the goats come into the picture. The school is purchasing goats, pigs, and chickens to teach the children how to care for these animals and to provide food for the school. These animals provide resources for the school to be able to care for more children and to teach more children about Jesus.

So you see, goats can be used to do missions! Christians are using goats to help feed hungry people and tell them about Jesus. God's Word in Isaiah 58:10 tells us, _____.
(Read the verse.) This is saying that when we spend our time feeding the hungry and caring for people who are suffering, those people and others will notice. They will see that there is something unique about the way we care for them, and then we can tell them about Jesus.

Prayer
God, we thank You for meeting the needs of these children and families with animals. Thank You that these people are learning about Jesus.

Making It Stick

Let the children discuss what it might be like to have and care for farm animals. *(If any children in the class actually live on a farm or ranch, ask them to tell about some of the things they do each day to care for their animals.)* Ask children to imagine how they could use animals and what it might be like to use them to support the family. Encourage children to draw a picture of their imagined farm. Include in the picture how they would use their farm to minister to others. Pray for the families in the ministries that you heard about.

Making It Personal

Memorize Isaiah 58:10. What does this verse mean to you?

What are some things that you can do to help the hungry in your community?

Making It Home

As a family, explore www.readtofeed.org and www.ricksonline.org. Afterward, talk about what you have learned. Discuss how Christ followers could use projects like these to minister to others. Do a mission action project in your community to minister to the hungry.

Missional Extra—Taking It Further

Visit www.wmu.com/VolunteerConnection/International and www.ricksonline.org for more information about these ministries.

"THUMB"

Missional Message: God wants us to have a biblical worldview.

Missional Challenge:
"Do not conform any longer to the pattern of this world, but be transformed by the renewing of your mind. Then you will be able to test and approve what God's will is—his good, pleasing and perfect will."
—Romans 12:2

What Is Needed: World airline route map or another world map, yarn and tacks if desired, poster with a thumb and the acronym "THUMB" imprinted on it

Making It Real
(Show a map. An international airline trip map would be an excellent resource for this lesson since it already has routes drawn on it. If you use another type of map, draw lines or use yarn and tacks to represent

routes that airplanes travel the world daily as they move people from country to country.)

This map represents how the people of the world are moving from place to place throughout the world. People are able to travel to even the farthest places in about a day. There are people from every country visiting or living in the United States and in other nations. These people bring different cultures with them. With the different cultures come different ways that people see the world. This is called a *worldview*. Your worldview comes from what you believe.

Christians have a *biblical worldview*. Having a biblical worldview simply means that what we believe about God, how we live, and how we treat others are based on our understanding of the Bible.

There are five major non-Christian worldviews. They are tribal, Hindu, unreligious, Muslim, and Buddhist. An easy way to remember these is the acronym THUMB, (a mnemonic which stands for these largest groups of nonChristians, and is referenced in many books urging children to pray for them, including the *Kids Around the World* series produced by Caleb Resources and in *Prayer-Saturated Kids: Empowering and Equipping Children in Prayer* by Cheryl Sacks and Arlyn Lawrence.)

(Hold up your thumb. Now say, "THUMB." Show the children a poster with a thumb and the acronym for THUMB printed on it. Show them each letter and have them repeat the words with you.) "THUMB: tribal, Hindu, unreligious, Muslim, and Buddhist. You also can remember these worldviews by counting them off with your fingers." *(Demonstrate starting with your thumb.)*

It is important that we understand that a biblical worldview is very different from other worldviews. The Bible says in Romans 12:2, _____. *(Read that verse.)* We need to understand what the Bible says, so we can learn from and follow the one true God. Then when we learn things from the world we live in, we will be able to know whether those ideas and worldviews are Christian or not.

Prayer
God, thank You for giving us the Bible. Help us to have a worldview based on the Bible.

Making It Stick

Read through the following worldviews. The source for the following information on worldviews is Ergun Mehmet Caner's book, *When Worldviews Collide: Christians Confronting Culture*. Help the children determine which worldviews are Christian and which are not. Encourage children to go to the Bible to find answers to their questions and to learn the truth about God. *(Note the verses we have added after the stated worldview, which can help to refute the falsehoods of these beliefs and which may be of special help if children get confused by any of these points.)*

- People are part of God (Hindu)—Isaiah 53:6a, Isaiah 55:8.
- Respect Jesus as a prophet (Muslim)—John 3:16, 1 Corinthians 8:6.
- People are saved by works (Every belief system except Christianity)—Ephesians 2:8.
- After a person dies, the person is reincarnated into another human or object or animal (Hindu/Buddhist)—Hebrews 9:26-28.
- Peace is found through meditation (Buddhist)—John 14:1, John 14:27.
- Natural disasters are works of evil spirits (Tribal)—Exodus 9:13-15, Isaiah 13:11, Ephesians 6:12, 1 John 5:19. *(Be very careful with this one—verses often can seem to contradict themselves if you are not prepared to respond to the question of how a loving God can allow or cause disasters to befall people.)*
- God does not exist (Unbeliever)—Psalm 14:1, Psalm 53:1.

Have the children think of other things they hear about God. Help them to understand which beliefs are biblical and which are not. Understanding what is *biblical* is an advanced, abstract concept that may be more difficult for concrete-thinking younger children to understand.

Making It Personal

Memorize Romans 12:2.

This week, ask your friends to share with you what they believe to be true about God. Look in the Bible to see if what the Bible says about God agrees with your friends' ideas about Him. Ask an adult who knows the Bible to assist you in finding the answers. A good online source is biblegateway.com or crosswalk.com, where you can look up verses, key words, and topics.

Making It Home
Have each family member make a list of the things they believe about God. Collect all the lists. Then research the Bible to see if the thoughts on the list are true or false. Discuss the fact that we need to test what we hear, believe, or see about God to be sure it is what the Bible says, before we accept those things as truth. The Bible is truth.

Missional Extra—Taking It Further
Teaching resources for the THUMB acronym can found at www.takeitglobal.org, www.navpress.com, or www.calebresources.org.

THUMB: Tribal Peoples

45

Missional Message: God wants us to know and be controlled by His Holy Spirit.

Missional Challenge:
"You, however, are controlled not by the sinful nature but by the Spirit, if the Spirit of God lives in you. And if anyone does not have the Spirit of Christ, he does not belong to Christ."
—Romans 8:9

What Is Needed: Bible, pictures of animist/tribal people, and Internet access

Making It Real

(*Show a picture of a group that is animist/tribal in its beliefs.*) This group of people have beliefs that we call *animistic*. We will refer to people who practice those beliefs as "tribal." (*If you taught the THUMB message earlier, review the THUMB acronym's meaning.*)

Tribal people are found all over the world. In North America, many Native American Indian groups have an animist worldview.

What do tribal people believe? Tribal people believe spirits are in the powers of nature. For example, if a storm comes and destroys your home, tribal people would think it was the work of an evil spirit. They believe spirits live in everything. Some are evil spirits that do bad things, but some are good spirits. Tribal people do things that they believe make the spirits happy, like making sacrifices and wearing special jewelry to protect them. They live in fear of the spirits.

They do believe there is a creator god. They think that God created the world, but that He is distant and is not interested in what happens to them.

What does the Bible say? Romans 8:9: *"You, however, are controlled not by the sinful nature but by the Spirit, if the Spirit of God lives in you. And if anyone does not have the Spirit of Christ, he does not belong to Christ."* There is only one Spirit of God, and He is the Holy Spirit. The Holy Spirit lives in Christians and guides them to follow God.

Another Bible verse, Romans 8:15, promises us that Christians are free from fear by their close relationship with the Father: *"For you did not receive a spirit that makes you a slave again to fear, but you received the Spirit of sonship. And by him we cry, 'Abba, Father.'"* "Abba" means something like "Daddy!" God is not distant. He is with us through His Holy Spirit. God calls us His adopted children. He is our Father.

Prayer
God, thank You for being with us. Thank You that there is no fear in You.

Making It Stick
If you have Internet access (which is desirable for this lesson), show the children information you pull up about a tribal group with information found at www.joshuaproject.net. There is a wealth of information on the Web site along with detailed statistics. Point out differences between the tribal beliefs and biblical truth. Or you can share the book,

Window on the World: When We Pray God Works by Daphne Spraggett with Jill Johnstone.

Making It Personal
Memorize Romans 8:15.

Write a letter to God telling Him how grateful you are that He is not a distant God, but a God that is with us every moment of the day.

Making It Home
Adopt a tribal people group and pray for that group regularly. The Joshua Project offers helpful information on people groups. As a family, learn about one or more people groups, and pray for them daily.

THUMB: Hindu Beliefs

46

Missional Message: God gives us eternal life through Jesus.

Missional Challenge:
"Just as man is destined to die once, and after that to face judgment, so Christ was sacrificed once to take away the sins of many people; and he will appear a second time, not to bear sin, but to bring salvation to those who are waiting for him."
—Hebrews 9:27–28

What Is Needed: Bible and picture of a Hindu god (may be found at images.google.com, searching for "Hindu god"), posters that illustrate the three ways to peace taught by Hinduism

Making It Real

(*Show a picture of a Hindu god.*) Believers in the Hindu religion make up about 14 percent to 15 percent of the world population. More than 1 billion people claim to be Hindu. Hindu believers are prominent in

India and Pakistan, and are quickly growing in number in the United States and Europe.

What do Hindus believe? Hindus believe that a part of God is in everything. They believe Brahma is the highest being or God. There are thousand of smaller gods that are part of the Brahma. Hindus believe that after they die, they come back as other persons or animals. If they were good in their past lives, they get better lives in the next one. If they were bad in their past lives, they might come back as animals.

Their goal is to reach a state of peace. Hindus believe that there are three ways to obtain eternal peace or what we could call "salvation." *(Hold up the posters that illustrate the three following characteristics as you explain them.)*

- The first is the **way of works.** They believe they can gain peace by purifying their thoughts and deeds through rituals, ceremonies, and acts of self-denial.
- The second way to peace and salvation is the **way of knowledge.** Hindus study and meditate so they can gain spiritual understanding called *enlightenment*.
- The third way is the **way of devotion.** This is a combination of works and knowledge where they spend time in deep thoughts focused on the god or gods they worship.

What does the Bible say? The Bible teaches something very different from what believers in Hinduism accept as true. Hebrews 9:27–28 states,

> "Just as man is destined to die once, and after that to face judgment, so Christ was sacrificed once to take away the sins of many people; and he will appear a second time, not to bear sin, but to bring salvation to those who are waiting for him."

This Bible passage says that a person dies only once and, at that point, faces God. We each get just one life to live. We do not get a series of chances until we get it right.

As for the way to obtain peace or salvation, Hebrews 9:27–28 tells us the way to salvation or eternal peace is through Jesus Christ. There is only one way—Jesus Christ.

Prayer
God, thank You for Jesus. You have shown us that He is the way to You, to eternal peace, and to salvation for each one of us.

Making It Stick
People who practice the Hindu religion are very open to following multiple gods and will accept Jesus as another god while keeping their Hindu beliefs and practices. Have children role-play how they would talk to a Hindu about Jesus being the *only* way to salvation and eternal peace.

Making It Personal
Memorize Hebrews 9:27–28.

Have you ever thought that being good would earn you points with God? It certainly is not wrong to want to please God and be devoted to Him or to meditate on Scripture. However, Hebrews 9:27–28 gets to the real solution. No matter what we do, we cannot save ourselves. Only Jesus can save us. Each night this week, read Hebrews 9:27–28 a couple of times, and think about what it means.

Making It Home
Watch a family-friendly movie that refers to India. For example, *Brother Bear* or *Jungle Book*, or another you can find. Afterward, discuss references to Hinduism and research what the Bible says.

THUMB: Unreligious People

Missional Message: God wants all people to know Him and believe in Him.

Missional Challenge:
"For since the creation of the world God's invisible qualities—his eternal power and divine nature—have been clearly seen, being understood from what has been made, so that men are without excuse."
—Romans 1:20

What Is Needed: Bible, papers, and markers

Making It Real
(*Pretend to pull something from your pocket and hide it in your hand.*) I have a symbol in my hand to show you what unreligious people believe about God. (*Bring your hands apart quickly to reveal there is nothing there.*) That is right. They do not believe that God exists. Sometimes these people are referred to as *atheists* or *skeptics*. Atheists believe

there is no God. They believe that all religious beliefs are wrong.

Unreligious people assume that having faith in God is a weakness. And they look to science to explain how life began and exists. They trust in education, money, and their country's leaders to provide for their needs. In a way, they believe they are their own gods.

What does the Bible say? Romans 1:20 says, *"For since the creation of the world God's invisible qualities—his eternal power and divine nature—have been clearly seen, being understood from what has been made, so that men are without excuse."* This verse says there is a God. We know this by looking at His creation. The beauty of nature and the miracle of the human body all reveal God.

Philippians 4:13 states, *"I can do everything through him who gives me strength."* Believing in God and trusting Him gives us strength to do anything and everything that God wants us to do. Now, that does not sound like a weak person at all! Actually, believing in God is a great source of strength for Christ followers.

Prayer
God, thank You for being an amazing God, and thank You for the strength You provide.

Making It Stick
Ask children, "Have you ever thought that God does not exist? How do we know that He exists?" Have children draw a picture in full color showing how they know God exists. Encourage them to share their drawing with a friend outside of church.

Making It Personal
Memorize Romans 1:20.

Read Genesis 1. Think about how God took great care to create the world and how only God could do what He did. Read Romans 1:20. How does what this verse says about God echo the story of God's creation of the world in Genesis 1? This week, look around you and take notice of what an amazing job God did creating the world.

Making It Home

Talk together as a family about how believing that God made the world colors a person's outlook on life. An example might be whether one believes people are made in the image of God or that they are simply like animals. Our beliefs influence how we treat the sick, the dying, even the unborn. If there are older children in the family they can help with parents' research about the theory of intelligent design and Darwinism online, or at a library, or in your children's school books. Discuss as a family how these belief systems differ. Determine which system more accurately supports a biblical worldview.

THUMB: Muslim Beliefs

48

Missional Message: God is personal.

Missional Challenge: *"See that what you have heard from the beginning remains in you. If it does, you also will remain in the Son and in the Father. And this is what he promised us—even eternal life."*
—1 John 2:24–25

What Is Needed: Bible, scale, paper, and pencils or markers.

Making It Real

When I say the word *Muslim,* what do you think? (*Let children provide some answers.*) Most Muslim believers would be very sad to find out that other people do not like them. The Muslims would say that they are followers of a religion called Islam. There are between 1.4 and 1.7 billion Muslims worldwide. Followers of Islam are the largest religious group immigrating to the United States.

What do Muslims believe? The Muslim faith, or Islam, began in 610 A.D. with a man called Muhammad. On his fortieth birthday, he had a seizure and a vision. He believed they were from God. He preached that Christians had abandoned the truth of God. He took parts of the Bible and rewrote them and added his own teachings to those parts to create a new book called the Koran (*or Qur'an, as it is commonly spelled today*). The Koran is the holy book to Muslims.

Muslims must follow five rules for daily living called the "Five Pillars of Islam":

- Confess "There is no god but Allah. Muhammad is the messenger of Allah."
- Pray five times a day facing Mecca, birthplace of Muhammad.
- Give a percentage of one's income to charity.
- Fast during the Islamic holiday of Ramadan.
- Travel to Mecca in honor of Muhammad.

One expert on the religion of Islam says, "To make it to Heaven, they must do more good than bad, think more good than bad, and be more good than bad. They must be 51 percent righteous at the time of death to make it into paradise." (*Show the children a scale. Label the scale "good" on one side and "bad" on the other side.*) What a Muslim believes is like this scale: the moment you die, if you have a little more on the good side, you are going to heaven. Muslims try to build up the good side by having daily prayer rituals and by doing good works.

What does the Bible say? The New Testament book of 2 Peter 1:20–21 says,

> *"Above all, you must understand that no prophecy of Scripture came about by the prophet's own interpretation. For prophecy never had its origin in the will of man, but men spoke from God as they were carried along by the Holy Spirit."*

This means the words of the Bible are from God—they are complete and unchangeable. Muhammad was incorrect in his belief that man had made mistakes speaking of God in the Bible, because the Bible is from God, not man.

The Apostle John also tells us, *"See that what you have heard from the beginning remains in you. If it does, you also will remain in the Son and in the Father. And this is what he promised us—even eternal life"* (1 John 2:24–25). God has not changed. What He has promised is true. When we ask Jesus to be the Lord over our lives, He fulfills His promise and sends His Holy Spirit to be with us, and He gives us eternal life. Christianity is not about how good or bad we are. Christianity is about to whom we know and we have given our lives to. Christians have a relationship with Jesus; they know Him personally.

Prayer
God, thank You for giving us Your truth through the Bible and thank You for giving us salvation through Jesus.

Making It Stick
Ask the children to share their ideas about Islam and Muslims. (*Perhaps a child who prints well could write the misconceptions on a dry wipe board or blackboard.*) Then say, "Many Muslims believe that all US citizens are Christians. Do you think the U.S. culture (TV, clothing, movies, and music) defines what it means to be a Christian?" Discuss how both Christians and Muslims have unrealistic ideas about each other. Read John 3:16, and have the children list ways they can share God's love with Muslims.

Making It Personal
Memorize 1 John 2:24–25. This verse says to apply, believe, and accept what you have learned. When we accept Jesus, He becomes a part of our lives. He is not a God far off who requires us to do certain acts to be good in His sight. Jesus wants us to follow Him each day with joy because we love Him. Think of every day with Jesus as a new journey. On a piece of paper, draw a line. Think of this timeline as your life's journey from the beginning until now. Put arrows or marks at points on the line to represent special times in your life and label them with descriptions of the events that you are remembering. Include special times with God along the timeline.

Making It Home
Discuss why Muslim women cover their heads in public. Muslim

women cover themselves to show reverence to their god. (*There is a wealth of information online that helps to provide perspective, both Muslim and non-Muslim, on this issue.*)

Discuss ways that your family shows reverence to God.

Also, make a point this week to pray for the Muslim families you know or see. Encourage family members to make an extra effort to greet or talk to Muslims, keeping in mind that Muslims do not typically talk directly with strangers of the opposite sex. Build relationships with Muslims to share God's love with them.

THUMB: BUDDHIST BELIEFS

49

Missional Message: Jesus is the only way to God.

Missional Challenge:
"Jesus answered, 'I am the way and the truth and the life. No one comes to the Father except through me.'"
—John 14:6

What Is Needed: Bible, picture of Buddhist prayer flags, paper, and markers

Making It Real

How many of you have gone to an Asian restaurant and have seen an altar with a statue of a sometimes plump man sitting with his legs crossed who looks as if he is praying or thinking? These statues help to form many people's ideas about Buddha, the founder of Buddhism.

There are an estimated 350 million Buddhists worldwide. Since the 1970s, the Buddhist religion has grown 2,000 percent in the United States alone. It is popular on university campuses and in Hollywood.

What do Buddhists believe? About 2,500 years ago, a Hindu prince named Siddhartha Gautama became unhappy that people suffer, live, and die. So he set out to discover truth, or enlightenment. He meditated for 49 days until he received enlightenment. Gautama then began teaching. People called him *Buddha*, which meant the "enlightened one."

Gautama taught that to be free from suffering, life, and death, people had to follow something called a "Noble Eightfold Path" *(write them on a blackboard or dry wipe board if possible)* that required them to do eight things:

- Be kind.
- Do not harm any living things.
- Live in a right way.
- Tell the truth.
- Do not think of self.
- Think about others.
- Understand suffering.
- Meditate.

What does the Bible say? In John 14:6, Jesus said, *"I am the way and the truth and the life. No one comes to the Father except through me."* God wants us to live, not to to stop existing after we die. Jesus says that He is the life. In Jesus, we should want to live both on earth *and* in heaven.

Second, though the Noble Eightfold Path does have some good ideas about how to live, those ideas are just good ideas. They are not the truth that will lead you to God. Jesus is the only way to God. The Bible teaches the only complete truth for us to believe.

Prayer
God, thank You that Jesus is our way, truth, and life. Thank You for revealing Jesus to us in the Bible.

Making It Stick
At many Buddhist temples, there are hundreds—even sometimes a thousand—prayer flags flying in the wind (search online for "prayer

flag" at images.google.com and print some of them prior to class if possible). Buddhists believe that the prayer flags carry their prayers to the farthest part of the universe. Christians believe our prayers go straight to God. Have the children draw a flag and write "Pray for Buddhists" on the flag. Encourage them to remember to pray for Buddhists to find Jesus every time children see a flag.

Making It Personal
Memorize John 14:6.

Buddhists are thinkers. They believe they can think and work their way through suffering, life, and death. The ways they live are good, but they depend on themselves rather than on God. What does John 14:6 say about the way, truth, and life and depending on Jesus?

Making It Home
Take your family to a restaurant that you know has a statue of Buddha. Ask the owner or manager what the statue of Buddha represents to him or her. Look around the room. What other things do you see that may or may not reflect Buddhism? When you return home, discuss what you saw and heard. Consider returning often to the restaurant to get to know the workers. Pray that God will provide an opportunity for you to share Jesus with them.

Moldova

Missional Message: God uses ordinary people who are willing to spread the good news.

Missional Challenge:
"The Lord's message rang out from you not only in Macedonia and Achaia—your faith in God has become known everywhere."
—1 Thessalonians 1:8a

What Is Needed: Bible and world map, copy of *Maria* Magazine if available.

Making It Real
(*Use the map to show the children where the country of Moldova is located.*) Moldova is a tiny country. It is located between Romania and Ukraine. There are 4.3 million people in Moldova. It was formerly part of the communist Soviet Union. Being a communist country meant that the government made it illegal for people in Moldova to

worship God. Today Moldova is a country where people have freedom of religion and people are now allowed to worship God there.

Today the country is very poor. It is one of the poorest countries in Europe. It has many social and political problems because of poverty. However, despite all the problems, Christians there are finding joy in Jesus and sharing that joy with others. In fact, some Christians in Moldova are telling the world about Jesus.

One believer who is making a difference is Olga Molcan.* Olga became a believer when she was 14, when it was illegal to be a Christian in the Soviet Union. She followed God, even when it was dangerous to believe in and trust Jesus. Olga married a pastor and had a family. In 1991, the Soviet Union ceased to exist. This gave Christians the freedom to worship Jesus.

Soon after the fall of the Soviet Union, Olga was invited to a meeting where Christians around the world came together to worship God. She met women from North America who worked at an organization called Woman's Missionary Union®. She was invited to visit their office in Birmingham, Alabama. When Olga saw all the missions education resources that WMU offered, she broke down in tears. At that moment, she felt God leading her to create a magazine for Russian-speaking women. In less than six months, she published a magazine called *Maria*. Today, *Maria* is sent all over the Russian-speaking world to teach women about Jesus and to encourage them to share their faith with others.

Olga is teaching Russian women throughout the world, including women who are now in the United States. Olga has a passion for God and His mission for the world. She is inspiring women to follow Jesus and share His love with others.

First Thessalonians 1:8*a* says, *"The Lord's message rang out from you not only in Macedonia and Achaia—your faith in God has become known everywhere."* Olga is an example of this: a believer, with very little resources, experiencing God's grace and sharing His message with the world.

Prayer
God, thank You for using ordinary people willing to spread Your Word and love.

Making It Stick
Initiate discussion with this statement: "If the government said tomorrow that we can no longer come to church or believe in Jesus, what would we do?" Have the children think of ways that we could worship God, fellowship with other believers, and share Jesus with others even if we could not meet in a church building.

Making It Personal
Memorize 1 Thessalonians 1:8a.

Question yourself: If it were dangerous to be a Christ follower, would I still follow Jesus? When you attend church this week, thank God for the freedom to worship that we enjoy. Pray for the people of the world who are not free to believe in Jesus or worship Him.

Making It Home
This week, have the family pretend that it is illegal to be a Christian. For example, hide the Bibles from view, take down anything in your house that would give you away as Christians, do not use Christian words, close the curtains when you are praying, pray in secret when you eat out, sneak into church or have a house church meeting, and such. At the end of the week, discuss how others can tell we are Christians. Is it hard or easy to hide being a follower of Jesus?

Missional Extra—Taking It Further
A serious issue in Moldova is human trafficking. People are being abducted and sold into slavery and shipped all over the world—even to the United States. For more information about human trafficking, visit www.salvationarmyusa.org/trafficking. Think about what we as followers of Christ can do to put a stop to this crime against humanity. Is there something specific that God is leading you to do?

---

*From the author's experience with Olga in Moldova

Indonesia

Missional Message: God shows us His amazing work.

Missional Challenge:
"Everyone was amazed and gave praise to God. They were filled with awe and said, 'We have seen remarkable things today.'"
—Luke 5:26

What Is Needed: Bible, poster, picture of Doors of Aceh and purse from www.worldcraftsvillage.com

Making It Real

In December 2004, a terrible earthquake and tsunami occurred in Southeast Asia. It killed many people and left almost 1 million people homeless. The hardest hit area was Banda Aceh, Indonesia. Banda Aceh was the place where Indonesian Islam began. Today, Indonesia has the largest Islamic population in the world—even more than in the Middle East, where Muhammad was born. Before the tsunami, Banda

Aceh was known for extreme Islam and civil war. Not many foreigners visited Banda Aceh.

Within hours of the tsunami, the world learned of Banda Aceh and the devastation of the community. The world responded. In less than a week, groups from every country and religion were in Aceh trying to figure out how to help.

Christians began to pray and go. One group from the United States went in April 2005 to help do relief work. The group found the people of Aceh to be friendly, kind, and grateful. The group bought purses from Aceh that had a beautiful pattern on the outside called the Doors of Aceh (www.worldcraftsvillage.com features a picture of beautiful purses and totes decorated with the design. You can print in advance and show to the children).

When they returned to the US, a member of the group gave a purse to a friend at WorldCrafts℠. The person at WorldCrafts found a way to sell the purses in the US. Today, the money raised from the sale of these purses not only supports thousands of employees and their families in Aceh, but the purses also serve as a reminder to pray that the doors of Aceh and Indonesia will be open to Jesus.*

(*Read Luke 5:26.*) Let's pray that God will continue to do amazing things in Aceh.

Prayer

God, we pray that You will do incredible things in the lives of the people of Aceh.

Making It Stick

Draw a set of large double doors on a poster board to symbolize the Doors of Aceh. Ask the children to write in prayer requests for the people of Aceh on the doors. Pray with the children asking Him to open the doors of the hearts of the people of Aceh. Hang the poster.

Making It Personal

Memorize Luke 5:26.

Write a list of some of the amazing things that you have seen God do in your neighborhood and community. This week pray that God will show you how He is working in your community and around the world. Be ready to be amazed!

Making It Home

God is doing amazing work around the world through His people. Teach your family about how He is working through other countries and groups featured at www.worldcraftsvillage.com.

Missional Extra—Taking It Further

The Doors of Aceh products can be purchased at: www.worldcraftsvillage.com. These are excellent witnessing tools.

*Story based on author's personal experience.

South Africa 52

Missional Message: God is our hope.

Missional Challenge:
"He has delivered us from such a deadly peril, and he will deliver us. On him we have set our hope that he will continue to deliver us."
—2 Corinthians 1:10

What Is Needed: Bible, paper, and pencils, dry wipe board or blackboard, pictures of Living Hope Centre and some of the people there, if available from their online gallery.

Making It Real
(The following story is from a 2007 WorldCrafts video.) I have a story to share with you about a South African woman. There was a young mother who had just had a baby. Soon after the baby was born, the hospital did blood tests on the mother and baby. The mother was told that they were both HIV positive. HIV is a sickness that leads to AIDS

and eventually death. The mother was so upset she named her child Aliko Ithemba, which means "no hope." A chaplain, a Christian who provides spiritual help at the hospital, saw the name of the baby and asked the mother why she would name her child something so terrible. The mother told her how her life and now the life of her baby was hopeless because they had HIV.

The chaplain told the mother about Jesus. The mother became a Christian. The chaplain encouraged the mother to join a support group at Living Hope Community Centre. The mother joined the group and said for the first time that she found hope. She changed her baby's name to "Lelethu," which means, "The Lord is my hope" in her language.

The Bible says in 2 Corinthians 1:10 that our hope is God. *(Read the verse.)* He is the young mother's hope, and the baby's hope, too. This young mother found hope through the ministry of Living Hope. *(Show pictures if you can, as indicated below.)* In 1999, Fish Hoek Baptist Church in South Africa, under the leadership of its pastor, John Thomas, began the Living Hope Community Centre to help families affected by HIV. The church wanted to give these families the hope of Jesus. Living Hope also ministers to children in several communities to teach them about Jesus. In 2006, the Centre had almost three thousand children, ages 5 to 16, attend its children's clubs. (See http://www.livinghope.co.za/?go=services-programs.)

Prayer
God, thank You for giving the people of South Africa hope through Living Hope Community Centre.

Making It Stick
Make two columns on a dry wipe board or blackboard. Label the first column "No Hope." Have the children tell you about times in life when there seems to be no hope. Encourage them to share situations they have seen around them and global issues they may be aware of. In the next column, write "The Lord Is Our Hope." Have the children think of how we can look to God for hope in these and all situations. If time permits, have the children write a letter to the children who

attend Living Hope Community Centre's clubs, encouraging them to find hope in Jesus.

Making It Personal
Memorize 2 Corinthians 1:10.

God said He would be with us in the hard times and give us hope. God wants us to share His hope with others. Think about someone you know who may need to hear this promise. Write that person a letter or draw a picture of encouragement that will give him or her hope. Include the Scripture verse.

Making It Home
Teach your children that no one deserves AIDS and that God wants us to share His hope with children and adults living with HIV/AIDS. To learn more about HIV/AIDS, visit *www.purposedriven.com* and click on the HIV/AIDS link. Pray about getting involved and/or supporting HIV/AIDS ministries in your community.

Missional Extra
For more information about Living Hope, visit www.livinghope.co.za. The mother in this story is one of the jewelry makers that create the Living Hope crafts featured at www.worldcraftsvillage.com.

Resources

Recommended Books for Parents
1001 Ways to Introduce Your Child to the Bible by Kathie Reimer
Families on Mission: Ideas for Teaching Your Preschooler to Love, Share, and Care by Angie Quantrell
Joining Children on their Spiritual Journey by Catherine Stonehouse
Love Notes in Lunchboxes by Linda Gilden
Missions Moments: Foundational Messages and Activities for Children by Mitzi Eaker
Stirring Up a World of Fun: International Recipes, Wacky Facts and Family Time Ideas by Nanette Goings
Teaching Your Child How to Pray by Rick Osborne.
We Can Do That! 100+ Ways Families Can Be On Mission by Tonya Heartsill
Window on the World by Daphne Spraggett with Jill Johnstone
For more books recommended by Mitzi, visit www.MitziEaker.com

Missions Resources for Children's Leaders
Children in Action Curriculum www.childrensmissions.com

Girls in Action Curriculum www.gapassport.com

Christ Followers (Multi-generational downloadable curriculum) www.wmustore.com

Exploring God's World Reading Club www.childrensmissions.com

Children's Ministry Day. www.childrensmissions.com

Products to teach preschoolers and children about missions www.wmustore.com

Missions Camping resources www.wmustore.com

The following Web sites were active as of 2008. New Hope Publisher or Mitzi Eaker cannot guarantee that these sites do not contain offensive materials or are still active. We encourage adults to check these and all Web sites before guiding a child to view sites.

Web Sites for Leaders and Parents (as featured in this book)
www.worldvision.org
www.billygrahamcenter.com
www.bread.org

www.childrensmissions.com
www.cia.gov/cia/publications/factbook
www.joshuaproject.com
www.livinghope.co.za
www.peoplegroups.info
www.praykids.com
www.purposedriven.com
www.ricksonline.org
www.salvationarmyusa.org/trafficking
www.samaritianspurse.org/default.asp
www.takeitglobal.org
www.uofnkona.edu
www.wmu.com/volunteerconnection/internation
www.worldcraftsvillage.com
www.worldmap.org

Web Sites on Poverty

www.kidscount.org/census (US secular site)
www.poverty.us (United States secular site)
www.un.org/millenniumgoals (The world secular site)

Fun Christian Sites for Children

http://bigidea.com/ (Veggietales)
www.childrensmissions.com and *www.gapassport.com (Woman's Missionary Union)*
www.highlightskids.com (Highlights Magazine)
www.kidzplace.org (North American Mission Board)
www.kidsonmission.org (International Missions Board)
www.whitsend.org (Focus on the Family)
www.upperroom.org/pockets/ (Pockets)
www.wonderzone.com/activities/ (Child Evangelism Fellowship)
www.wycliffe.org/kids/home.htm (Wycliffe)

Also, Mitzi would love to hear how you have used the book to teach children about missions and missional living.

Topical Index

AIDS	168
Animist	45
Buddhism	49
Children's Sunday	24, 26, 27
Christmas	11
Church Starting	14, 38
Croatia	43
Discipleship	12, 14, 21, 26, 29, 31, 35
Easter	13
Father's Day, Mother's Day, Grandparents Day	1
Fellowship/Community/Church	2, 25, 40
Friendship	32
Heaven	17
Hinduism	46
Islam	48
Indonesia	52
Love God, Love Others	22, 23
Liberia	43
Missions	19, 33, 34, 35, 36, 38, 40, 41, 42, 50
Missionary	7, 37 38, 40, 43
Ministry	18, 19, 24, 26, 42, 43
Moldova	50
Operation Christmas Child	42
Paul	14
People Groups	33, 44, 45, 46, 47, 48, 49
Salvation	13, 20
Sanctity of Human Life	24
Stewardship:	
Life	24, 25, 27
Earth	3
Friends	32
Money	28, 29
Speech	30

THUMB 142–159
Time 26
South Africa 52
Speaking, Testimony 30, 31
Witnessing/Evangelism 9, 10, 13, 14, 31, 33, 34, 39

Biblical Worldview:
    Obeying God 4
    Trusting God 5
    Depending on God 6
    Following God 7, 12
    God with us 8, 9
    Knowing God 21
    Loving God 22

Holy Spirit 16, 34
Youth With A Mission 41
WMU 43
Worldcrafts Ministries 50, 51

New Hope® Publishers is a division of WMU®, an international organization that challenges Christian believers to understand and be radically involved in God's mission. For more information about WMU, go to www.wmu.com. More information about New Hope books may be found at www.newhopepublishers.com. New Hope books may be purchased at your local bookstore.

More Parenting Resources from New Hope

Setting Up Stones
*A Parent's Guide to Making Your
Home a Place of Worship*
Martha and Greg Singleton
ISBN: 1-59669-219-7

Families on Mission
*Ideas for Teaching Your
Preschooler to Love, Share, and Care*
Angie Quantrell
ISBN: 1-56309-991-8

Mommy Pick-Me-Ups
Refreshing Stories to Lighten Your Load
Edna Ellison and Linda Gilden
ISBN: 1-59669-218-9

Baby Boot Camp
*Basic Training for the First Six
Weeks of Motherhood*
Rebecca Ingram Powell
ISBN: 1-56309-820-2

Available in bookstores everywhere

For information about these books or any New Hope product,
visit www.newhopepublishers.com.